OPPOSING VIEWPOINTS® SERIES

AIDS

Other Books of Related Interest:

Opposing Viewpoints Series
Human Rights
Medicine
Sexually Transmitted Diseases

Current Controversies Series
Health Care
Homosexuality

At Issue Series
Heroin
Sexually Transmitted Diseases

"Congress shall make no law . . . abridging the freedom of speech, or of the press."

First Amendment to the U.S. Constitution

The basic foundation of our democracy is the First Amendment guarantee of freedom of expression. The Opposing Viewpoints Series is dedicated to the concept of this basic freedom and the idea that it is more important to practice it than to enshrine it.

OPPOSING VIEWPOINTS® SERIES

AIDS

Viqi Wagner, Book Editor

GREENHAVEN PRESS

An imprint of Thomson Gale, a part of The Thomson Corporation

THOMSON

GALE

Detroit • New York • San Francisco • New Haven, Conn. • Waterville, Maine • London

Christine Nasso, *Publisher*
Elizabeth Des Chenes, *Managing Editor*

© 2008 The Gale Group.

Star logo is a trademark and Gale and Greenhaven Press are registered trademarks used herein under license.

For more information, contact:
Greenhaven Press
27500 Drake Rd.
Farmington Hills, MI 48331-3535
Or you can visit our Internet site at http://www.gale.com

Articles in Greenhaven Press anthologies are often edited for length to meet page requirements. In addition, original titles of these works are changed to clearly present the main thesis and to explicitly indicate the author's opinion. Every effort is made to ensure that Greenhaven Press accurately reflects the original intent of the authors. Every effort has been made to trace the owners of copyrighted material.

Cover photograph reproduced by permission of freephotos.com

ISBN-13: 978-0-7377-3731-8 (hardcover)
ISBN-10: 0-7377-3731-X (hardcover)
ISBN-13: 978-0-7377-3732-5 (pbk.)
ISBN-10: 0-7377-3732-8 (pbk.)

Library of Congress Control Number: 2007934882

Contents

Chapter 3: How Can the Spread of AIDS Be Controlled?

Chapter 4: How Should AIDS Be Treated?

Why Consider Opposing Viewpoints?

> *"The only way in which a human being can make some approach to knowing the whole of a subject is by hearing what can be said about it by persons of every variety of opinion and studying all modes in which it can be looked at by every character of mind. No wise man ever acquired his wisdom in any mode but this."*
>
> *John Stuart Mill*

In our media-intensive culture it is not difficult to find differing opinions. Thousands of newspapers and magazines and dozens of radio and television talk shows resound with differing points of view. The difficulty lies in deciding which opinion to agree with and which "experts" seem the most credible. The more inundated we become with differing opinions and claims, the more essential it is to hone critical reading and thinking skills to evaluate these ideas. Opposing Viewpoints books address this problem directly by presenting stimulating debates that can be used to enhance and teach these skills. The varied opinions contained in each book examine many different aspects of a single issue. While examining these conveniently edited opposing views, readers can develop critical thinking skills such as the ability to compare and contrast authors' credibility, facts, argumentation styles, use of persuasive techniques, and other stylistic tools. In short, the Opposing Viewpoints series is an ideal way to attain the higher-level thinking and reading skills so essential in a culture of diverse and contradictory opinions.

In addition to providing a tool for critical thinking, Opposing Viewpoints books challenge readers to question their own strongly held opinions and assumptions. Most people form their opinions on the basis of upbringing, peer pressure, and personal, cultural, or professional bias. By reading carefully balanced opposing views, readers must directly confront new ideas as well as the opinions of those with whom they disagree. This is not to simplistically argue that everyone who reads opposing views will—or should—change his or her opinion. Instead, the series enhances readers' understanding of their own views by encouraging confrontation with opposing ideas. Careful examination of others' views can lead to the readers' understanding of the logical inconsistencies in their own opinions, perspective on why they hold an opinion, and the consideration of the possibility that their opinion requires further evaluation.

Evaluating Other Opinions

To ensure that this type of examination occurs, Opposing Viewpoints books present all types of opinions. Prominent spokespeople on different sides of each issue as well as well-known professionals from many disciplines challenge the reader. An additional goal of the series is to provide a forum for other, less known, or even unpopular viewpoints. The opinion of an ordinary person who has had to make the decision to cut off life support from a terminally ill relative, for example, may be just as valuable and provide just as much insight as a medical ethicist's professional opinion. The editors have two additional purposes in including these less known views. One, the editors encourage readers to respect others' opinions—even when not enhanced by professional credibility. It is only by reading or listening to and objectively evaluating others' ideas that one can determine whether they are worthy of consideration. Two, the inclusion of such viewpoints encourages the important critical thinking skill of objectively evaluating an author's credentials and bias. This evaluation will illuminate an author's reasons for taking a particular stance on an issue and will aid in readers' evaluation of the author's ideas.

It is our hope that these books will give readers a deeper understanding of the issues debated and an appreciation of the complexity of even seemingly simple issues when good and honest people disagree. This awareness is particularly important in a democratic society such as ours in which people enter into public debate to determine the common good. Those with whom one disagrees should not be regarded as enemies but rather as people whose views deserve careful examination and may shed light on one's own.

Thomas Jefferson once said that "difference of opinion leads to inquiry, and inquiry to truth." Jefferson, a broadly educated man, argued that "if a nation expects to be ignorant and free . . . it expects what never was and never will be." As individuals and as a nation, it is imperative that we consider the opinions of others and examine them with skill and discernment. The Opposing Viewpoints series is intended to help readers achieve this goal.

David L. Bender and Bruno Leone,
Founders

Introduction

> *"The impact of the AIDS movement on biomedical institutions in the United States has been impressive and conspicuous.*
>
> —Steven Epstein,
> Impure Science: AIDS, Activism,
> and the Politics of Knowledge

A thorough exploration of the subject of AIDS is incomplete without considering the role that AIDS activism has played throughout the history of the epidemic. The influence of AIDS activism, in fact, has reached far beyond AIDS-related issues. As early as 1992, the *Washington Post* attested to the comprehensive impact on American healthcare in an article titled "AIDS Activism Improves Medicine":

> Among policymakers, physicians and legal experts, this has become a familiar story. Ten years of AIDS activism, they say, has had a profound impact on U.S. regulation, law and society far beyond the immediate world of those infected with the HIV virus. . . . [AIDS activism] also has changed the way medical science is conducted, the relationship between doctor and patient, the way Americans talk about sex, the way drugs are regulated and the way civil rights law is written.

Similarly, as researchers and policy-makers become more aware of the global reach of the AIDS epidemic, many note the essential role of activists in organizing international prevention and treatment programs. Political scientists Raymond A. Smith and Patricia D. Siplon document the rise and success of this second wave of AIDS activism in *Drugs into Bodies: Global AIDS Treatment Activism*. They credit activists with altering government policies, securing funding for treatment, and making medicines available to those who had little access to them before.

On the American scene, it was the June 5, 1981 edition of the Centers for Disease Control and Prevention's (CDC) *Morbidity and Mortality Weekly Report (MMWR)* that first drew attention to the unusual situation of five young men in Los Angeles, all active homosexuals, who were suffering from rare diseases usually limited to severely immunosuppressed patients. Later that year when patients numbered in the hundreds, it became clear that a full-blown epidemic was in effect involving an illness that came to be known as Acquired Immunodeficiency Syndrome, or AIDS. For two years, skyrocketing numbers of deaths due to AIDS and tallies of newly infected patients left most people petrified with astonishment. By 1983, however, a group of people with AIDS, or "PWAs," fought the inertia and organized a self-empowerment campaign, asserting that they should have more control over their own treatment. Three years later, the AIDS Coalition to Unleash Power, or ACT UP, was born, largely in reaction to growing anti-AIDS phobia in the public and to governmental inaction around funding AIDS treatment and research. According to the 2007 article "ACT UP at 20" in the *Nation*, "ACT UP would revolutionize AIDS research and treatment, as well as inject new life into the gay movement and infuse the tactic of direct action with its own style of theatrical militancy."

One of ACT UP's main goals was made into a slogan: "Drugs into Bodies." Activists called for more government funding to develop new drugs to treat AIDS and to research cures. They also demanded faster drug testing and affordable prices for treatments that initially were outrageously expensive. Underscoring the need for widely available medications would remain central to the ACT UP agenda for years to come, but ACT UP also initiated massive public "safer-sex" education to stop the spread of AIDS and fought to protect the privacy and rights of PWAs who were threatened with mandatory testing and discrimination in insurance, employment, and housing. Additional ACT UP issues included addressing the specific needs of women and ethnic/racial minorities, securing food and housing for PWAs, and advocating for education and treatment programs for drug users in danger of becoming infected through needle-sharing.

Perhaps ACT UP is best known for organizing spectacular direct actions in order to achieve its many victories for PWAs. Over the years, activists stormed the Federal Drug Administration, the National Institutes of Health, and the CDC to protest their sluggish response to AIDS. Appalled at the $8,000-a-month price tag for the treatment drug AZT when it was first made available by the pharmaceutical giant Burroughs-Wellcome, activists occupied their offices and then shut down the trading floor of the New York Stock Exchange to successfully force the company to reduce the price of the drug AZT by 20 percent. In addition to such dramatic actions, ACT UP painstakingly trained many of its members to become citizen-experts in subjects such as virology and patient law in order to participate in medical conferences and policy meetings. Their interventions eventually empowered patients of all kinds to be considered a fundamental part of medical decision-making and research agendas. Many historians agree that while other AIDS activist efforts have come and gone in the United States, none have had the impact of ACT UP. "Today," concludes the *Nation* in its retrospective article, "anyone who gains access to an experimental drug before it's approved, or takes a life-saving medicine that was fast-tracked through the FDA—indeed, anyone engaged in the struggle for health-care—is indebted to ACT UP's audacity and vision."

Although in recent years ACT UP has taken a less central role in the domestic AIDS response, many former ACT UP members have become a driving force for global treatment access. For example, ACT UP alums founded Health Global Access Project, or Health GAP, which uses similar disruptive activist's tactics to campaign for drugs and any other resources necessary to sustain treatment for people with HIV/AIDS across the globe. Among many achievements, Health GAP has successfully influenced U.S. trade policies related to treatment drugs, pressured multinational corporations to provide AIDS treatment to workers, and exposed the price-gouging activities of U.S. pharmaceutical companies. Whether in the American context or the global realm, says Lawrence Gostin, executive director of the American Society of Law and Medicine in Boston, "you can look at all of the major cutting-edge issues in health law and ethics and you can see how AIDS has had an impact. It is the lens we use to examine all the critical issues."

The push-and-pull tensions among dissimilar interest groups in the history of AIDS activism provide one lens for examining the controversies in the global AIDS epidemic. AIDS intersects many areas of the social fabric, including science, education, law, race and ethnicity, religion, and sexuality. Divergent constituencies promote different viewpoints about the status of the AIDS epidemic, the causes of AIDS, the appropriate prevention strategies to stem the spread of AIDS, and the best treatment programs for PWAs. These topics and others are discussed in *Opposing Viewpoints: AIDS* in order to stimulate critical thinking about one of the most devastating health issues in the modern world.

CHAPTER 1

What Is the Status of the Global AIDS Epidemic?

Chapter Preface

Women and AIDS

Examining the global AIDS epidemic can be overwhelming. In December 2006, the World Health Organization (WHO) estimated that 39.5 million people worldwide were living with HIV, and that 4.3 million people were newly infected that year. Broad-spectrum statistics illustrate the growing threat of AIDS to the entire human race, but they can also draw attention away from the way the AIDS epidemic is hitting some subpopulations harder than others. One of those subpopulations is women.

When the epidemic first came to light in the United States in the 1980s, few women and girls were thought to be infected with HIV. Largely, this was due to the way HIV was spreading most quickly in gay male communities. It was also partly because of the limited knowledge about HIV transmission, which caused the medical establishment to overlook women who had been infected, whether through injection drug use or sexual contact. The initial perception that AIDS was a male disease, and especially the assumption that HIV infection happened only during sex between men, prevented doctors and researchers from including women in patient studies, drug trials, prevention campaigns, and treatment programs.

In recent years, more policy makers and medical experts have acknowledged that women must be included in AIDS programs, from research to treatment. More thorough inclusion of women has revealed startling results. In June 2007, the Centers for Disease Control and Prevention (CDC) reported that U.S. women accounted for one fourth of all new HIV/AIDS diagnoses. Women made up 23 percent of the estimated 421,873 people living with AIDS, and over 85,000 women have died since the beginning of the epidemic. Moreover, some females are at a greater risk than others. African American women are diagnosed with AIDS at twenty times the rate of white women. In fact, the rates for African American women are higher than the rates for all men, with the exception of African American men. Hispanic women also bear the burden of AIDS more than white, Asian American, and Native American women. Age is another important factor in statistics in the United States. The largest number of HIV/AIDS diagnoses for women of all ethnicities was for females aged 15–39.

Similar data emerges upon examining the AIDS epidemic globally, especially in developing regions such as sub-Saharan Africa. By the 1990s, WHO was reporting that over five million people in Africa were infected with HIV, at a ratio of five men to three women. Such numbers destroyed the myth that AIDS was a problem of gay men exclusively. By 2002, WHO reported that 42 million Africans were living with HIV/AIDS and 19.2 million of them were women. Almost 50 percent of new and existing adult victims were female.

Some analysts believe that political and economic inequalities related to race, ethnicity, and gender contribute to the increased vulnerability of women in the current AIDS epidemic. The CDC cites high risk factors for women in the United States such as unemployment, financial dependence on male partners, and low self-esteem coupled with the need to feel loved by a male figure. The CDC notes that more African American and Hispanic women live in poverty in the United States than any other women. In the book *Women in the New Millennium*, African AIDS researchers Mokgadi Moletsane and Mark DeLancey argue that

> the wide-spread phenomenon that women are economically, politically, legally and socially in weaker positions than men is a major explanation of the increasing number of women infected by HIV in Africa and elsewhere where heterosexual relations are the main mode of transmission.

Statements like these prompt some to conclude that, to be effective, AIDS prevention and treatment programs must address the gender inequalities and traditional practices that limit women's autonomy and make them particularly susceptible to AIDS.

"*The number of people living with HIV*
continues to grow, as does the number
of deaths due to AIDS."

The Global AIDS Epidemic
Is a Growing Threat

Joint United Nations Programme on HIV/AIDS
and World Health Organization

The Joint United Nations Programme for HIV/AIDS (UNAIDS)
is a collaboration of ten UN organizations, including the United
Nations Children's Fund (UNICEF), the World Health Organi-
zation (WHO), and the World Bank, founded in 1996 to coordi-
nate global efforts to track, treat, and prevent AIDS. In the fol-
lowing viewpoint, UNAIDS reports the latest statistics on the
spread of HIV and AIDS mortality to show that globally, despite
improved access to prevention programs and antiretroviral drugs,
an estimated 4.3 million people were newly infected with HIV,
and 2.9 million people died of AIDS in 2006. Between 2004 and
2006, according to UNAIDS, the number of people living with
HIV increased in every region in the world and now totals nearly
40 million.

As you read, consider the following questions:

1. According to UNAIDS and WHO, two-thirds of all people with HIV live in sub-Saharan Africa; in this region, which countries are hardest hit and where is HIV infection rising suddenly after years of decline?

2. Which population groups globally are at highest risk of HIV infection, according to the UNAIDS 2006 report?

3. How does the main mode of HIV transmission differ in Central Asia, sub-Saharan Africa, and Europe, according to UNAIDS researchers?

Promising developments have been seen in recent years in global efforts to address the AIDS epidemic, including increased access to effective treatment and prevention programmes. However, the number of people living with HIV continues to grow, as does the number of deaths due to AIDS. A total of 39.5 million [34.1 million–47.1 million] people were living with HIV in 2006—2.6 million more than in 2004. This figure includes the estimated 4.3 million [3.6 million–6.6 million] adults and children who were newly infected with HIV in 2006, which is about 400,000 more than in 2004.

In many regions of the world, new HIV infections are heavily concentrated among young people (15–24 years of age). Among adults 15 years and older, young people accounted for 40% of new HIV infections in 2006.

High-Risk Regions

Sub-Saharan Africa continues to bear the brunt of the global epidemic. Two thirds (63%) of all adults and children with HIV globally live in sub-Saharan Africa, with its epicentre in southern Africa. One third (32%) of all people with HIV globally live in southern Africa and 34% of all deaths due to AIDS in 2006 occurred there.

Declines in national HIV prevalence are being observed in some sub-Saharan African countries, but such trends are currently neither strong nor widespread enough to diminish the epidemic's overall impact in this region.

Almost three quarters (72%) of all adult and child deaths due to AIDS in 2006 occurred in sub-Saharan Africa: 2.1 million [1.8 million–2.4 million] of the global total of 2.9 million [2.5 million–3.5 million]. Overall sub-Saharan Africa is home to an estimated 24.7 million [21.8 million–27.7 million] adults and children infected with HIV—1.1 million more than in 2004.

In the past two years, the number of people living with HIV increased in every region in the world. The most striking increases have occurred in East Asia and in Eastern Europe and Central Asia, where the number of people living with HIV in 2006 was over one fifth (21%) higher than in 2004.

The 270,300 [170,000–820,000] adults and children newly infected with HIV in Eastern Europe and Central Asia in 2006 showed an increase of almost 70% over the 160,000 [110,000–470,000] people who acquired HIV in 2004. In South and South-East Asia, the number of new HIV infections rose by 15% in 2004–2006, while in the Middle East and North Africa it grew by 12%. In Latin America, the Caribbean and North America, new infections in 2006 remained roughly the same as in 2004.

Globally, and in every region, more adult women (15 years or older) than ever before are now living with HIV. The 17.7 million [15.1 million–20.9 million] women living with HIV in 2006 represented an increase of over one million compared with 2004. In sub-Saharan Africa, for every ten adult men living with HIV, there are about 14 adult women who are infected with the virus. Across all age groups, 59% of people living with HIV in sub-Saharan Africa in 2006 were women. In the Caribbean, the Middle East and North Africa, and Oceania, close to one in every two adults with HIV is female. Meanwhile, in many countries of Asia, Eastern Europe and Latin America, the proportions of women living with HIV continue to grow.

Access to treatment and care has greatly increased in recent years, albeit from a very low starting level in many countries. Nevertheless, the benefits are dramatic. Through the expanded provision of antiretroviral treatment, an estimated two million life years were gained since 2002 in low- and middle-income countries. In sub-Saharan Africa alone, some 790,000 life years have been gained, the vast majority of them in the past two years of antiretroviral treatment scale-up. In Latin America, where wide-scale treatment provision began earlier, some 834,000 life years have been gained since 2002.

High-Risk Groups

The centrality of high-risk behaviour (such as injecting drug use, unprotected paid sex and unprotected sex between men) is especially evident in the HIV epidemics of Asia, Eastern Europe and Latin America. In Eastern Europe and Central Asia, for example, two in three (67%) prevalent HIV infections in 2005 were due to the use of non-sterile injecting drug use equipment. Sex workers and their clients, some of whom also inject drugs, accounted for about 12% of HIV infections.

Paid sex and injecting drug use accounted for a similar overall proportion of prevalent HIV infections in South and South-East Asia. Excluding India, almost one in two (49%) prevalent HIV infections in 2005 were in sex workers and their clients, and more than one in five (22%) infections were in injecting drug users. A small but significant proportion of infections (5%) were in men who have sex with men. In Latin America, in contrast, one in four (26%) of the HIV infections in 2005 were in men who have sex with men, while 19% were in injecting drug users. Although HIV prevalence in sex workers is relatively low in this region, they and their clients accounted for almost one in six (17%) HIV infections.

Although the epidemics also extend into the general populations of countries in those regions, they remain highly concentrated around specific population groups. This highlights the need to focus prevention, treatment and care strategies effectively on population groups that are most at risk of HIV infection.

Latest Developments in Africa

Almost 25 million people are living with HIV in sub-Saharan Africa—63% of all persons with HIV globally. Considerable efforts have been made towards improving access to antiretroviral treatment in recent years. Nonetheless, 2.1 million [1.8 million—2.4 million] Africans died of AIDS in 2006—almost three quarters (72%) of all AIDS deaths globally.

Hardest-hit is southern Africa, where Zimbabwe remains the only country where national adult HIV prevalence has declined. The declining trend appears to be partly associated with behaviour changes dating back to the mid- to late-1990s.

Meanwhile, the HIV epidemics in Mozambique, South Africa, and Swaziland continue to grow. An estimated one in three (33%) adults in Swaziland was living with HIV in 2005—the most intense epidemic in the world. In South Africa, which in terms of sheer numbers has one of the world's largest HIV epidemics, prevalence of HIV among women attending public antenatal clinics was more than one third (35%) higher in 2005 than it had been in 1999. While HIV infection levels among young pregnant women appear to be stabilizing, they continue to increase among older women. The epidemic is having a significant impact. Death rates from natural causes for women aged 25–34 years increased fivefold between 1997 and 2004, and for males aged 30–44 they more than doubled. A large part of those increases is due to the AIDS epidemic.

In East Africa, where HIV infection levels have been lower than in the south of the continent, the general trend of a stabilizing or a declining HIV prevalence appears to be continuing. National HIV prevalence among pregnant women has declined in Kenya, as it has in Tanzania and, to a lesser extent, in Rwanda. In many other countries though, discrepant trends

HIV Is Increasing throughout the World				
	Adults and children living with HIV	Adults and children newly infected with HIV	Adult (15–49) prevalence (%)	Adult and child deaths due to AIDS
Middle East and North Africa				
2006	460,000	68,000	0.2%	36,000
	[270,000–760,000]	[41,000–220,000]	[0.1%–0.3%]	[20,000–60,000]
2004	400,000	59,000	0.2%	33,000
	[230,000–650,000]	[34,000–170,000]	[0.1%–0.3%]	[18,000–55,000]
East Asia				
2006	750,000	100,000	0.1%	43,000
	[460,000–1.2 million]	[56,000–300,000]	[<0.2%]	[26,000–64,000]
2004	620,000	90,000	0.1%	33,000
	[380,000–1.0 million]	[50,000–270,000]	[<0.2%]	[20,000–49,000]
Western and Central Europe				
2006	740,000	22,000	0.3%	12,000
	[580,000–970,000]	[18,000–33,000]	[0.2%–0.4%]	[<15,000]
2004	700,000	22,000	0.3%	12,000
	[550,000–920,000]	[18,000–33,000]	[0.2%–0.4%]	[<15,000]
North America				
2006	1.4 million	43,000	0.8%	18,000
	[880,000–2.2 million]	[34,000–65,000]	[0.6%–1.1%]	[11,000–26,000]
2004	1.2 million	43,000	0.7%	18,000
	[710,000–1.9 million]	[34,000–65,000]	[0.4%–1.0%]	[11,000–26,000]

TAKEN FROM: UNAIDS and WHO, "AIDS Epidemic Update: Special Report on HIV/AIDS," December 2006, p. 2.

are often being found at local levels. Meanwhile, new research indicates a possible erosion of the gains Uganda made against AIDS in the 1990s, and HIV prevalence has again been rising in some rural areas. A sudden increase in infection levels among pregnant women in 2005 in Burundi's capital, Bujumbura, could reverse the general, post-2000 decline in HIV prevalence in that country.

West and Central Africa's smaller epidemics show divergent trends. There are signs of declining HIV prevalence in urban parts of Burkina Faso, Côte d'Ivoire and Ghana, but in Mali the HIV epidemic appears to be growing. A recent development in sub-Saharan Africa is the emergence of injecting drug use as a potential factor in the HIV epidemics of several countries, notably those of Kenya and Tanzania (as well as Nigeria and South Africa).

Latest Developments in Asia

In Asia, national HIV infection levels are highest in South-East Asia, where combinations of unprotected paid sex and unprotected sex between men, along with unsafe injecting drug use, are the largest risk factors for HIV infection. HIV outbreaks among men who have sex with men are now becoming evident in Cambodia, China, India, Nepal, Pakistan,

Thailand and Viet Nam. In very few of these countries, national AIDS programmes adequately address the role of sex between men in the epidemics. HIV outbreaks are being found in Afghanistan and Pakistan, particularly among injecting drug users. High levels of use of non-sterile injecting equipment and other risk behaviours offer the HIV epidemic considerable scope for growth in these two countries.

The HIV epidemic in India is best described as a series of epidemics, widely varied with respect to prevalence levels, risk factors for infection and transmission patterns. Some of these epidemics appear to be stable or diminishing in parts of the south, while others are growing at a modest rate elsewhere. In China, where the authorities have greatly expanded the AIDS response, HIV is spreading gradually from most-at-risk populations (especially injecting drug users and commercial sex workers and clients) to the general population, and the number of HIV infections in women is growing.

Latest Developments in
North and South America

Latin America's epidemics remain generally stable, with Brazil in particular providing proof that a dual emphasis on prevention and treatment can keep an HIV epidemic under control. Outbreaks of the virus continue to be found among injecting drug users and men who have sex with men in most countries of South America. Although largely a hidden behaviour, sex between men likely accounts for as much as one tenth of reported HIV cases in the Caribbean. In that region, HIV prevalence remains stable in the Dominican Republic and has declined in urban parts of Haiti, but there are some localized indications that the epidemics in both countries could start to increase again if prevention efforts are not enhanced.

Racial and ethnic minorities in the United States of America continue to be disproportionately affected by the HIV epidemic, while Aboriginal people are over-represented in Canada's epidemic. There, as in Western and Central Europe, the main risk factor for HIV remains unprotected sex between men. HIV prevalence ranges between 10% and 20% among men who have sex with men in several countries in Western Europe, amid evidence of increased casual and unprotected sex in this population group. At the same time, approximately three quarters of heterosexually acquired HIV infections in Western and Central Europe are among immigrants and migrants. This fact underlines the need to adapt prevention, treatment, and care services so that they reach these populations.

The HIV epidemics in Eastern Europe and Central Asia are still relatively young, and they continue to grow—most strikingly in Ukraine, which has the highest HIV prevalence in all of Europe. There, as in the Russian Federation's expanding epidemic and in the smaller but growing epidemics of Tajikistan and Uzbekistan, the use of non-sterile injecting drug equipment remains the main mode of HIV transmission. The HIV epidemics in these regions are most greatly affecting young people; in the Russian Federation, for example, some 80% of people with HIV are younger than 30 years of age. In the Russian Federation and Ukraine, women (many of them less than 25 years old) bear a growing proportion of the HIV burden, accounting for more than 40% of new HIV diagnoses in 2005.

Inadequate HIV surveillance remains a hindrance in many countries—including Europe, the Caribbean, Central America, the Middle East and North Africa. This makes it difficult to discern precisely the patterns and trends of some HIV epidemics, and hinders the design and implementation of potentially effective responses. There are recent exceptions, among them Iran, which has acted on improved HIV information gathering by expanding its AIDS response among at-risk populations.

HIV and Sexual Behaviour
Trends Among Young People

In 2001, the United Nations' *Declaration of Commitment on HIV/AIDS* outlined a goal of reducing HIV prevalence by 25% in young people in the most-affected countries by 2005, in order to monitor progress in preventing new infections. Determining real time trends in HIV incidence, and in particular the impact of prevention programmes on HIV incidence—ideally requires longitudinal studies of large numbers of people. Given the practical difficulties of conducting such studies, it has been proposed to use HIV prevalence in young women aged 15–24 attending antenatal clinics as a proxy measure for incidence.

To assess progress towards this goal, countries in which national prevalence exceeds 3% were asked by the WHO/UNAIDS Working Group on Global HIV/AIDS and STI surveillance to participate in this endeavour.

HIV prevalence has declined since 2000/2001 in eight of 11 countries with sufficient data to analyze recent trends among young people. In Kenya, HIV prevalence among young pregnant women declined significantly, by more than 25%, in both urban and rural areas. Similar declines were evident in urban areas in Côte d'Ivoire, Malawi and Zimbabwe, and in rural parts of Botswana. Less prominent (and non-significant) declines were observed in urban Botswana, Burundi and Rwanda and in rural Tanzania and Zimbabwe. There was no evidence of a decrease in HIV infection levels among young people in Mozambique, South Africa or in Zambia.

Using results from national surveys conducted at least twice in the same country during the period 1992–2005, trends in behaviours among young people were assessed. In Kenya, behaviour trend data point to a significant reduction over time in the kinds of sexual behaviour that place people at risk of HIV infection. The proportion of young persons having sex with non-regular partners decreased in Haiti (men only),

Kenya and Malawi (young men and women), and Zambia (women only), but increased in Cameroon, and Uganda (women only). Meanwhile, condom use rates with non-regular partners seemed to increase in some of the surveyed countries, including Cameroon, South Africa, Tanzania and Uganda (young men and women), Malawi (young men only), and Kenya and Zambia (young women only). In a few countries, most notably Cameroon, there appeared to be simultaneous shifts towards both safer and high-risk behaviours—with increases in the percentages of young people who engage in high-risk sexual activities occurring alongside rising rates of condom use during casual sex with a non-regular partner, for example.

Unfortunately, relatively few countries were able to provide extensive behavioural trend data for young people, and many countries had insufficient or no data on HIV prevalence trends among young people—including some of the countries with exceptionally high HIV prevalence in southern Africa. This reinforces the need to expand HIV surveillance activities as a matter of urgency.

The future course of the world's HIV epidemics hinges in many respects on the behaviours young people adopt or maintain, and the contextual factors that affect those choices.

> "Figures [of AIDS cases] are estimates arrived at by basing very questionable statistical manipulations on what are often ludicrously small numbers."

The Global AIDS Epidemic Is Exaggerated

James P. Hogan

In the following viewpoint, James P. Hogan argues that the global AIDS epidemic is wildly exaggerated. He criticizes reporting agencies such as the Centers for Disease Control and the World Health Organization for boosting AIDS diagnoses by repeatedly redefining existing diseases as indicators of AIDS. Moreover, Hogan claims, nearly seventy non-AIDS-related conditions— even non-illnesses such as prior pregnancy—produce positive HIV tests, further inflating AIDS statistics. James P. Hogan is a British electronics engineer and the author of more than two dozen science fiction novels, including the Prometheus Award-winning The Multiplex Man.

As you read, consider the following questions:

1. According to the author, how did the way AIDS cases in Canada were reported show a dramatic increase when in fact total cases had decreased?

James P. Hogan, from *Kicking the Sacred Cow: Questioning the Unquestionable and Thinking the Impermissible*, Wake Forest, NC: Baen Books, 2004. Reproduced by permission.

2. In Hogan's view, why does an HIV-positive test result actually mean HIV-immune, not HIV-infected?

3. Mistaken clinical diagnoses of AIDS are based on symptoms actually caused by which other diseases, according to Hogan?

Statistics for new AIDS cases were always quoted [in the 1990s] as cumulative figures that could only get bigger, contrasting with the normal practice with other diseases of reporting annual figures, where any decline is clear at a glance. And despite the media's ongoing stridency about an epidemic out of control, the actual figures from the Centers for Disease Control (CDC), for every category, were declining, and had been since a peak around 1988. This was masked by repeated redefinitions to cover more diseases, so that what wasn't AIDS one day became AIDS the next, causing more cases to be diagnosed. This happened five times from 1982 to 1993, with the result that the first nine months of 1993 showed as an overall rise of 5% what would otherwise—i.e., by the 1992 definition—have been a 33% drop.

As of January 2003 the number of indicator diseases is 29. One of the newer categories added in 1993 was cervical cancer. (Militant feminists had been protesting that men received too much of the relief appropriations for AIDS victims.) Nobody was catching anything new, but suddenly in one group of the population what hadn't been AIDS one day became AIDS the next, and we had the headlines loudly proclaiming that heterosexual women were the fastest-growing AIDS group.

Deceptive Reporting Boosts AIDS Figures

A similar deception is practiced with percentages, as illustrated by figures publicized in Canada, whose population is around 40 million. In 1995, a total of 1,410 adult AIDS cases were reported, 1,295 (91.8%) males and 115 (8.2%) females. 1996 showed a startling decrease in new cases to 792, consisting of 707 males (89.2%) and 85 females (10.8%). So the number of adult female AIDS cases actually decreased by 26% from 1995 to 1996. Yet, even though the actual number decreased, because the percentage of the total represented by women increased from 8.2% in 1995 to 10.8% in 1996, the *Quarterly Surveillance Report* (August 1997) from the Bureau of HIV/AIDS and STD at the Canadian Laboratory Centre for Disease Control issued the ominous warning that AIDS cases among Canadian women had dramatically increased.

Meanwhile, a concerted campaign across the schools and campuses was doing its part to terrorize young people over the ravages of teenage AIDS. Again, actual figures tell a different story. The number of cases in New York City reported by the CDC for ages 13–19 from 1981 to the end of June 1992 were 872. When homosexuals, intravenous drug users, and hemophiliacs are eliminated, the number left not involving these risks (or not admitting to them) reduces to a grand total of 16 in an 11-year period. (Yes, sixteen. You did read that right.)

The correlation between HIV and AIDS that was repeatedly cited as proving cause was maintained by denying the violations of it. Obviously if HIV is the cause, the disease can't exist without it. (You don't catch flu without having the flu virus.) At a conference in Amsterdam in 1992, [molecular biologist Peter] Duesberg, who had long been maintaining that dozens of known instances of AIDS patients testing negative for HIV had been suppressed, produced 4,621 cases that he had found in the literature. The response was to define them as a new condition designated Idiopathic CD4+ Lymphocytopenia, or ICL, which is obscurese for "unexplained AIDS symptoms." The figures subsequently disappeared from official AIDS-counting statistics. . . .

An Epidemic of AIDS Testing

If HIV is virtually undetectable even in its alleged terminal victims, how do you test for it? You don't; you test for the antibody. What this means in principle is that a sample of the patient's blood is exposed to viral antigens derived from HIV prepared in vitro. If the blood plasma contains antibodies to that antigen, they will bind to it in a reaction that can be made visible by suitable means, termed Enzyme-Linked Immuno-Sorbent Assay, ELISA, for those who love quoting these things at cocktail parties.

Wait a minute. . . . Aren't antibodies part of the body's own defense equipment—that you either acquired from your mother, learned to make yourself at some time in life when you encountered the virus, or were tricked into making by a vaccine? If you have no symptoms of an illness and no detectable virus, but your system is supplying itself with antibodies, isn't this a pretty good description of immunity?

Yes—for any other disease, and if we were dealing with rationality. But this is the land of AIDS. The usual reason for antibody testing is as a check to see if somebody needs to renew their shots. Also, there are situations where testing for the antibody to a pathogen suspected of causing a condition can make sense, given the right circumstances. If a person is showing clinical symptoms that are known to be caused by that pathogen . . . and a test has been shown independently to identify an antibody specific to that pathogen, then testing for the antibody can be a convenient way of confirming the suspected disease without going through the rigmarole of isolation.

But none of this is true of HIV. It has never been shown to cause anything, nor has a likely explanation even been advanced as to how it could. What, then, if anything, does the "HIV test" mean?

A genuinely useful antibody test can confirm that an observed sickness is due to the microbe thought to be the culprit. A positive HIV result from somebody who is completely symptom-free, on the other hand, means either that the antibody has been carried from birth without the virus ever having been encountered, or that the virus has been successfully neutralized to the point of invisibility. So in this context, "HIV positive" means HIV-immune. Interpreting it as a prediction that somebody will die years hence from some unspecifiable disease makes about as much sense as diagnosing smallpox in a healthy person from the presence of antibodies acquired through childhood vaccination.

Testing for What?

The test can mean a lot of other things, too. The most common [test], known as ELISA, was developed in 1984 for blood screening. Now, when you're looking for contaminated blood, you want a test that's oversensitive—where anything suspect will ding the bell. If the positive is false, after all, you merely throw away a pint of blood; but if a false negative gets through, the consequences could be catastrophic. (Whether or not you're screening for is a real hazard isn't the issue here.) But the same test started being used for diagnosis. And when people are being told that a positive result means certainty of developing a disease that's inevitably fatal, that's a very different thing indeed.

Here are some of the other things that can give a positive result, which even some doctors that I've talked to weren't aware of: prior pregnancy; alcoholism; certain cancers; malaria antibodies; leprosy antibodies; flu vaccination; heating of blood sample; prolonged storage of the sample; numerous other viruses; various parasitic diseases; hepatitis B antibodies; rheumatoid arthritis. In fact, almost 70 other causes have been shown to be capable of causing a positive reaction that have nothing to do with AIDS conditions. In a mass screening in Russia in 1991, the WHO performed 30 million tests over a two-year period and found 30,000 positive results. Attempts to confirm these yielded around 300, of which 66 were actual AIDS cases.

UNAIDS Projections Are Wrong

Since 1985, Uganda's population has fully doubled. *Nightline*'s predicted 50 million dead Africans by the year 2000 proved to be 20 million in 2005, according to the UN's estimate. Further, "In sub-Saharan Africa, the region with the largest burden of the AIDS epidemic, data also indicate that the HIV incidence rate has peaked in most countries," according to the 2006 UNAIDS Report.

These figures are from an agency that itself has grossly exaggerated the world AIDS threat. For example, in 1998 it estimated that 12% of Rwandans age 15–49 were infected; now it says it's only 3%. Whoops. On the other hand, other agencies had estimated a horrific 30% of Rwandans were infected. According to James Chin, a former U.N. official who made some of the earliest global HIV estimates, such concocted figures are "pure advocacy."

Michael Fumento, "Understanding the AIDS Industry,"
National Post *(Canada), August 17, 2006.*

In addition to the tests being uncertain in that precisely what they measure has never been defined, and nonspecific in that many other factors can give the same result, they are not standardized. This means that no nationally or internationally accepted criteria exist for deciding what constitutes a positive result.

What people take as a death sentence on the basis of the things they've been told varies from one country to another, and even from one testing authority to another within the same country. The U.S. practice is to require a repeated positive result to an ELISA "Search" test, to be "Confirmed" by a test known as the HIV Western Blot (WB), which is supposed to be more accurate—although the UK won't use it because [of] the risk of misinterpretation due to cross-reactions.

However, despite the reassuringly suggestive terminology, the WB remains as nonspecific, since it tests for the same antigen proteins as ELISA (but separated out into bands, so it's possible to see which ones are causing the reaction) and has likewise never been verified against any gold standard. In fact, some authorities cite it as the "standard" for assessing ELISA. This is a bit like using one clock to check the accuracy [of] another, when neither has been verified to be correct in the first place. According to the WB interpretations handed down in different places, an HIV positive African would not be positive in Australia; a positive from the U.S. Multicenter AIDS Cohort Study 1983–1992 would not be positive anywhere else in the world, including Africa. The pamphlet supplied with the ELISA test kit from Abbott Laboratories states: "At present there is no recognized standard for establishing the presence or absence of antibodies to HIV-1 and HIV-2 in human blood." ...

The Export Industry: Africa and Asia

"Everybody knows," from the flow of government and UN agency handouts uncritically passed on by the media that Africa is being devastated by an AIDS epidemic running out of control, with cases counted in tens of millions. What they probably don't realize is that the figures are estimates arrived at by basing very questionable statistical manipulations on what are often ludicrously small numbers, for example, leftover blood samples in a village prenatal clinic. So when UNAIDS announces that 14 million Africans are AIDS victims, it doesn't mean that 14 million bodies have been counted, but that computers in Geneva have run a model with an assumed relationship between positive test results and AIDS deaths, and extrapolated the results to the population of the entire continent. Thus in 1987 the WHO reported 1 million cases of "HIV disease" in Uganda. Yet 10 years later, the cumulative number of AIDS cases actually reported was

55,000. Nobody knew what had happened to the other 945,000. There are strong financial and other pressures that encourage the reporting as AIDS of old diseases that have been endemic on the African continent throughout history. According to Dr. Harvey Bialy, an American with long experience in Africa, because of the international funds poured into AIDS and HIV work, "It has become a joke in Uganda that you are not allowed to die of anything but AIDS. . . . A friend has just been run over by a truck; doctors put it down as AIDS-related suicide."

Unlike the cases in New York and San Francisco, the conditions that are reported as AIDS in Africa affect both sexes equally, which should be an immediate indicator that what's being talked about in the two instances are not the same thing. This is hardly surprising, since "AIDS" in Africa is accorded a different definition. The unifying factor that makes all of the 30-odd disparate indicator diseases "AIDS" in the West is testing positive for antibodies claimed to be specific to HIV. But in Africa no such test is necessary.

Virus hunters armed with antibody test kits began descending on the continent in the mid-1980s because of three pointers possibly linking it [HIV] to AIDS: a now-discredited theory that HIV might have originated there; the presence in Africa of an AIDS-related sarcoma (although it had existed in Africa since ancient times); and the presence of a small number of native Africans among AIDS cases reported in Western countries. And sure enough, they began finding people who reacted positive. Furthermore, the numbers were distributed equally between the sexes—just what was needed to demonstrate that AIDS was indeed an infectious condition, which statistics in the West refused, obstinately, to confirm. However, in 1985 a different, "clinical" definition was adopted, whereby "AIDS" was inferred from the presence of prolonged fevers (a month or more), weight loss of 10 percent or greater, and prolonged diarrhea.

The problem, of course, is that attributing these symptoms to a sexually transmitted virus invites—indeed, makes inevitable—the reclassifying of conditions like cholera, dysentery, malaria, TB, [and] typhus, long known to be products of poverty and tropical environments. More insidious, funds and resources are withdrawn from the support of low-cost but effective traditional clinics and the provision of basic nutrition, clean drinking water, and sanitation, and directed instead on ruinously expensive programs to contain a virus that exists for the most part in WHO statisticians' computers. Since it's decreed that "AIDS is caused by HIV," cases diagnosed according to the above definition are attributed to HIV presumptively. But studies where actual tests have been conducted show up to a half as testing negatively—making "AIDS" a catch-all that arises from the loosely interpreted antibody testing.

For as we've seen, many factors that are common in most African regions, such as malaria, leprosy, parasitical infections, [and] TB, can also test positive. This is a particular problem in Africa, where the population carries a naturally high assortment of antibodies, increasing the probability of cross-reactions to the point of making any results worthless. A study in central Africa found that 70 percent of the reported HIV positives were false. Nevertheless, the official reports attribute all positives to HIV, making every instance automatically an AIDS statistic. Of the resulting numbers, every case not known to be a homosexual or drug abuser is presumed to have been acquired through heterosexual transmission, resurrecting tendencies to sexual stereotyping that go back to Victorian racial fantasies. Given the incentives of limitless funding, a glamorous crusader image, and political visibility, it isn't difficult to discern an epidemic in such circumstances. People in desperate need of better nutrition and sanitation, basic health care and education, energy-intensive industrial technologies and productive capital investment are instead lectured on their morals and distributed condoms.

Spreading Hysteria Around the World

With the hysteria in the West now largely abated (although at the time of writing—early 2003—a campaign seems to be gathering momentum, targeting blacks), the bandwagon has moved on to embrace other parts of the Third World too. This follows a pattern that was set in Thailand, where an AIDS epidemic was said to be raging in the early nineties. Now, it so happens that over 90% of the inhabitants of Southeast Asia carry the hepatitis B antibody. The figure for actual disease cases in this region populated by tens of millions was around 700 in 1991, and by 1993 it had grown to 1500 or so. Perhaps what the reports meant was an epidemic of AIDS testing. Just like the inquisitors of old, the more assiduously the witch hunters apply their techniques and their instruments, sure enough they find more witches.

| *"The severe health impacts of AIDS [in Africa] are well documented. But AIDS also affects countries' fundamental economic and social development."*

AIDS Is Devastating Africa

Robert Hecht, et al.

In the following viewpoint, Robert Hecht and fellow researchers at the International AIDS Vaccine Initiative in New York and at EASE International in Copenhagen assess the devastating economic, social, and medical effects of HIV/AIDS on sub-Saharan Africa. According to Hecht and his colleagues, these destabilizing effects include entrenched extreme poverty, the prospect that 20 percent of the population will be orphaned children by 2010, steeply rising maternal and child mortality rates, and the spread of malaria and tuberculosis (TB). Hecht cites studies that project widespread economic collapse under these conditions within three generations.

As you read, consider the following questions:

1. How does HIV/AIDS not only increase poverty in the present generation but escalate poverty in the next generation, according to the authors?

Robert Hecht, et al, "Putting It Together: AIDS and the Millennium Development Goals," *PLoS Medicine*, vol. 3, November 28, 2006. Reproduced by permission.

2. How has HIV/AIDS reduced both the demand for and the supply of education in sub-Saharan Africa, in Hecht's analysis?

3. According to Hecht and his colleagues, how much is the rate of TB infection rising annually in sub-Saharan Africa, and how much of that is attributable to HIV?

One of the most important and visionary global actions of recent years was the September 2000 commitment by 189 governments worldwide to "[make] the right to development a reality for everyone and to [free] the entire human race from want." The movement to achieve sustainable reductions across all dimensions of extreme poverty has reached an unprecedented level, with efforts primarily focused on and measured against the Millennium Development Goals [MDGs are eight UN goals addressing poverty, disease, hunger, education, and environmental sustainability].

To date, progress toward achieving these goals has been mixed: . . . most notably in sub-Saharan Africa, a large number of countries are far behind and appear unlikely to reach, or even come close to reaching, their goals for 2015.

The reasons for this are complex and often interlinked, but one stands out as a major overarching threat to development: HIV/AIDS, which kills more people than any other infectious disease and is the fourth-leading cause of death worldwide. The severe health impacts of AIDS are well documented. But AIDS also affects countries' fundamental economic and social development performance, and exerts detrimental effects on many of the other MDGs. AIDS will make it difficult if not impossible for many countries to achieve their MDG targets. . . .

HIV/AIDS Increases Poverty

Various studies, using a range of modeling techniques, argue that AIDS lowers national gross domestic product (GDP) growth by up to 1.5% annually. An analysis across 80 developing countries predicts that in a "typical" African country with 20% HIV prevalence, the rate of GDP growth would be 2.6% lower each year than it would have been in the absence of AIDS. At the end of a 20-year period, GDP would be 67% lower than it would have been in the absence of AIDS at the end of a 20-year period.

Households face revenue losses and heavy costs. Because of high medical costs, as well as other expenses, of HIV-related illness and death, and because AIDS often kills working-age adults, the epidemic has a significant impact at the household level. Studies from Thailand and South Africa show that poverty is higher among households affected by HIV and AIDS than among unaffected families.

A recent analysis of household data from Botswana, drawing on income and expenditure surveys, suggests that HIV/AIDS can be expected to lower average income per capita by 10% [by 2016]. It also shows that the income loss is twice as large among the poorest households as it is for the overall population, suggesting that extreme poverty will become entrenched because of HIV/AIDS. A similar correlation between AIDS deaths and declining household wealth was found in rural Kenyan households.

These effects will escalate over time. The long-term negative impact of AIDS can be expected to accelerate. Classic GDP growth models may fail to capture the negative long-term intergenerational effects of HIV/AIDS.

One analysis that models the impact of HIV/AIDS over three generations shows how AIDS could produce a progressive collapse of the economy. Declining family income forces parents to choose immediate consumption (e.g., food and medical expenditures) over long-term investments in the next generation's human capital (e.g., school fees). As a result, children of parents who die of AIDS have less human capital to pass on to their own children.

The steadily increasing number of orphans in developing countries indicates how severe this problem could become. In South Africa, only 29% of children are expected to be living with both parents at the end of the current decade. Nearly one-fifth of children will have lost both parents.

HIV/AIDS Worsens the Nutritional Status of Children

Worldwide, 53% of annual deaths among children under five are associated with malnutrition. In areas with a high prevalence of HIV, progress in reducing childhood malnutrition has been mixed, and there is growing evidence of an important link between child nutrition, food security, and HIV/AIDS. In one study of 44 sub-Saharan countries, HIV prevalence was significantly negatively correlated with increasing calorie and protein consumption.

Some data suggest that HIV/AIDS contributes to food crises in areas where HIV prevalence is high. For example, a study that examines the impact of the 2002 drought in southern Africa finds that in six affected countries, child nutrition rapidly deteriorated in the presence of high HIV prevalence. The proportion of underweight children rose from 5% to 20% in Maputo (1997–2002), with similar increases in other sub-Saharan regions. Changes were much smaller during non-drought periods and in areas with lower HIV prevalence.

AIDS also affects child nutrition through parental mortality. Orphaned children are less likely to receive adequate nutrition. For example, in the Kagera region of Tanzania, maternal orphans lost on average one standard deviation in height, while paternal orphans' height declined one-third of a standard deviation. A study from Kenya shows that weight-for-height scores in 2000 were almost 0.3 standard deviations lower for orphans. In Lesotho, almost 40% of children under four who had lost both parents were underweight, compared with 16% of non-orphans.

AIDS Compromises Efforts to Reach
Universal Primary Education

The AIDS epidemic can negatively affect both the demand for and supply of education. AIDS may prevent children from enrolling in school, or cause them to be taken out of school. It can also cause absenteeism and mortality of teachers and staff, lowering educational quality and preventing children from obtaining schooling.

AIDS reduces the demand for schooling. Children in areas affected by AIDS may drop out of school because they or their families cannot afford fees or supplies, or because their families increasingly rely on them to contribute economically to the household or to care for ill family members. In a study in the Kagera region of Tanzania, young children (seven to ten years of age) who lost their mothers had their schooling delayed, though enrollment of older children (11–14 years of age) was not affected. A survey in Indonesia found that 14% of children who had lost a parent dropped out of school between ages six and ten, whereas only 7% of non-bereaved children did. . . .

AIDS also hampers countries' abilities to supply education. In many countries, educational administrators face substantial challenges in replacing teachers who die. Even when replacement teachers are readily available, the death of a teacher imposes substantial costs (for temporary and permanent teacher replacement, as well as for training) on education systems.

AIDS Has a Negative Impact
on Child Mortality

Worldwide, approximately 10.6 million children under five died in 2003. More than 40% of these deaths occurred in Africa. . . . In five countries that currently have adult HIV prevalence rates above 10% (Zambia, South Africa, Zimbabwe,

Sub-Saharan Africa: The Highest Incidence of HIV/AIDS in the World

In 2006, almost two thirds (63%) of all persons infected with HIV are living in sub-Saharan Africa—24.7 million [21.8 million–27.7 million]. An estimated 2.8 million [2.4 million–3.2 million] adults and children became infected with HIV in 2006, more than in all other regions of the world combined. The 2.1 million [1.8 million–2.4 million] AIDS deaths in sub-Saharan Africa represent 72% of global AIDS deaths. Across this region, women bear a disproportionate part of the AIDS burden: not only are they more likely than men to be infected with HIV, but in most countries they are also more likely to be the ones caring for people infected with HIV. . . .

Provision of antiretroviral therapy has expanded dramatically in sub-Saharan Africa: more than one million [930,000–1.15 million] people were receiving antiretroviral treatment by June 2006, a tenfold increase since December 2003 (WHO/UNAIDS, 2006). Scale-up efforts have been especially strong of late in a few countries, including Botswana, Kenya, Malawi, Namibia, Rwanda, South Africa, Uganda and Zambia.

However, the sheer scale of need in this region means that a little less than one quarter (23%) of the estimated 4.6 million [4 million–5.4 million] people in need of antiretroviral therapy in this region are receiving it (WHO/UNAIDS, 2006).

UNAIDS and WHO, "AIDS Epidemic Update: Special Report on HIV/AIDS," December 2006.

Botswana, and Swaziland), under-five mortality not only failed to decline between 1990 and 2003, it actually increased during that period.

Though AIDS contributes only modestly to global child mortality, the negative effects of HIV/AIDS are significant in high-prevalence areas. For instance, one analysis estimates that by 2015, up to 90% of under-five deaths in Botswana will be directly or indirectly caused by HIV/AIDS. Where the prevalence of HIV continues to increase in young women—as in many countries in sub-Saharan Africa—this effect will grow.

AIDS increases child mortality directly and indirectly. The vast majority of children living with HIV acquired the virus through perinatal transmission. And 60% of children with HIV die before their fifth birthday. In this manner, AIDS directly accounted for about 570,000 child deaths in 2005.

Child mortality can be attributed to AIDS even when HIV is not the direct cause of death, since children are made vulnerable to a range of economic and social "injuries" caused by their parents' illness and death. Maternal HIV status is a strong predictor of child survival, regardless of a child's HIV status. Several studies have shown that children born to mothers with HIV are approximately three times more likely to die than children born to mothers not infected with HIV. The effect of AIDS on child mortality is increasing. An analysis of HIV-related risk of death before age five in 42 sub-Saharan African countries estimates that in 1999, HIV accounted for 7.7% of under-five mortality, up from 2% in 1990. Another study estimates that in 2002, nearly 10% of all under-five deaths in sub-Saharan Africa could be attributed to HIV/AIDS. . . .

HIV/AIDS Worsens Maternal Health

Each year, more than 500,000 women die from pregnancy and childbirth-related complications, and at least 10 million suffer serious injuries or disabilities. More than 80% of these deaths occur in sub-Saharan Africa and South Asia.

HIV/AIDS can significantly increase maternal mortality ratios. Evidence suggests that suppressed immunity causes higher risks of prenatal and childbirth complications including miscarriage, anemia, postpartum hemorrhage, and puerperal sepsis, in addition to increasing the chances of dying from indirect causes during and after pregnancy, such as malaria or pneumonia.

Thus, maternal mortality ratios for women who are HIV positive can be substantially higher than for those who do not have HIV. For example, in Malawi and Zimbabwe, surveys suggest that the risk of pregnancy-related death is eight to nine times higher in women who are HIV positive. When HIV prevalence rates among pregnant women increased 10-fold between 1991 and 2001 in these countries, overall maternal mortality increased 1.9 and 2.5 times, respectively, likely as a result of this heightened risk. A similar study in Rakai, Uganda, found the rate of maternal deaths of women who are HIV positive to be more than three times the rate of women who do not have HIV.

A study in South Africa shows that the proportion of maternal deaths due to indirect infections (including HIV) increased from 23% to 31% over the period 1998–2001, making these infections the most significant causes of maternal mortality. In high-prevalence areas, this effect can substantially skew the population-wide maternal mortality ratio.

HIV Exacerbates the Effects of Malaria

Recent studies suggest that HIV has significant effects on the incidence of malaria. HIV-induced immunodeficiency may decrease the immune response against malarial infection, and indeed, the risk of parasitemia and illness has been inversely correlated to CD4 cell counts.

HIV co-infection in areas where malaria transmission is intense primarily increases the risk of parasitemia and clinical malaria in adults, and clinical malarial fever in children (although the evidence supporting a link between HIV infection and clinical malarial fever is stronger in adults than in children). In unstable malaria regions, in which transmission is intermittent and unpredictable, high HIV prevalence results in significantly higher malaria morbidity and mortality.

Clinical studies have also shown that HIV affects the incidence of malaria and disease progression in pregnant women. Increased rates of peripheral and placental parasitemia, higher parasite densities, and higher incidence of malaria, anemia, febrile illnesses, and adverse birth outcomes have been documented with HIV and malaria co-infection.

Infection with HIV also affects the treatment and prophylaxis of malaria. Antimalarial therapy works best in individuals with some previous immunity to malaria, so the immune suppression associated with HIV infection may decrease the response to antimalarial therapy.

HIV/AIDS Undermines Global Efforts to Control TB

The epidemics of HIV and TB are closely intertwined. Of the 40 million individuals who are HIV positive worldwide, it is estimated that nearly one-third are also infected with TB. Because of HIV-related immunosuppression, individuals with HIV who carry the TB bacillus are more susceptible to active TB than carriers who are HIV negative.

The risk of acquiring TB doubles soon after HIV infection, and increases during subsequent years. One study estimates that 9% of the 8.3 million new adult TB cases worldwide in 2000 were directly attributable to HIV. In addition, HIV infection makes it harder to treat active TB successfully.

Thus, TB rates are actually increasing in high-HIV-prevalence areas of sub-Saharan Africa and the spread of HIV in sub-Saharan Africa is primarily responsible for driving the number of active TB cases upward by 6% each year. A recent review on progress toward reaching the MDGs argues that the AIDS epidemic represents the greatest emerging threat to TB control.

> "[The AIDS epidemic] has begun to ebb in much of East Africa and has failed to take off as predicted in most of West Africa."

The Prevalence of AIDS in Africa Is Overstated

Craig Timberg

Estimates of HIV/AIDS cases in Africa by international monitoring agencies, primarily the Joint United Nations Programme on HIV/AIDS (UNAIDS), are too high by as much as 700 percent, journalist Craig Timberg reports in the following viewpoint. More accurate national studies have forced UNAIDS to steadily revise its estimates of HIV infection among working-age adults downward; for example, in Rwanda, from 12.75 in 1998, to 11.2 percent in 2000, to 8.9 percent in 2002, to 5.1 percent in 2004, to 3 percent in 2006. Timberg cites studies that show AIDS is a major health problem in parts of Africa but not nearly the continent-wide catastrophe once predicted. Craig Timberg is a staff writer for the Washington Post *foreign desk based in Johannesburg, South Africa.*

Craig Timberg, "How AIDS in Africa Was Overstated," *The Washington Post*, April 6, 2006. www.washingtonpost.com. Copyright © 2006 *The Washington Post*. Reprinted with permission.

As you read, consider the following questions:

1. What two factors account for the inaccuracy of UNAIDS estimates, according to Timberg?

2. According to the author, how do World Bank analyst David Wilson and other researchers dispute UNAIDS claims that the number of new HIV cases in Africa is rising?

3. How do inaccurate estimates of HIV infection affect international intervention and treatment programs, according to the author?

Researchers said nearly two decades ago that the tiny country [of Rwanda] was part of an AIDS Belt stretching across the midsection of Africa, a place so infected with a new, incurable disease that, in the hardest-hit places, one in three working-age adults were already doomed to die of it.

But AIDS deaths on the predicted scale never arrived here, government health officials say. A national study illustrates why: The rate of HIV infection among Rwandans ages 15 to 49 is 3 percent, according to the study, enough to qualify as a major health problem but not nearly the national catastrophe once predicted.

The data suggest the rate never reached the 30 percent estimated by some early researchers, nor the nearly 13 percent given by the United Nations in 1998.

The study and similar ones in 15 other countries have shed new light on the disease across Africa. Relying on the latest measurement tools, they portray an epidemic that is more female and more urban than previously believed, one that has begun to ebb in much of East Africa and has failed to take off as predicted in most of West Africa.

An AIDS Belt: Only in Southern Africa

Yet the disease is devastating southern Africa, according to the data. It is in that region alone—in countries including South

Africa, Botswana, Swaziland and Zimbabwe—that an AIDS Belt exists, the researchers say.

"What we know now more than ever is southern Africa is the absolute epicenter," said David Wilson, a senior AIDS analyst for the World Bank, speaking from Washington.

In the West African country of Ghana, for example, the overall infection rate for people ages 15 to 49 is 2.2 percent. But in Botswana, the national infection rate among the same age group is 25.3 percent. And in the city of Francistown, 45 percent of men and 69 percent of women ages 30 to 34 are infected with HIV, the virus that causes AIDS.

Most of the studies were conducted by ORC Macro, a research corporation based in Calverton, Md., and were funded by the U.S. Agency for International Development, other international donors and various national governments in the countries where the studies took place.

Taken together, they raise questions about monitoring by the U.N. AIDS agency [UNAIDS], which for years overestimated the extent of HIV/AIDS in East and West Africa and, by a smaller margin, in southern Africa, according to independent researchers and U.N. officials.

"What we had before, we cannot trust it," said Agnes Binagwaho, a senior Rwandan health official.

Broad Estimates of HIV Are Wrongly Based on Incidence Among Pregnant Women

Years of HIV overestimates, researchers say, flowed from the long-held assumption that the extent of infection among pregnant women who attended prenatal clinics provided a rough proxy for the rate among all working-age adults in a country. Working age was usually defined as 15 to 49. These rates also were among the only nationwide data available for many years, especially in Africa, where health tracking was generally rudimentary.

The new studies show, however, that these earlier estimates were skewed in favor of young, sexually active women in the urban areas that had prenatal clinics. Researchers now know that the HIV rate among these women tends to be higher than among the general population.

The new studies rely on random testing conducted across entire countries, rather than just among pregnant women, and they generally require two forms of blood testing to guard against the numerous false positive results that inflated early estimates of the disease. These studies also are far more effective at measuring the often dramatic variations in infection rates between rural and urban people and between men and women.

UNAIDS Estimates Are Far Too High

UNAIDS, the agency headed since its creation in 1995 by Peter Piot, a Belgian physician, produced its first global snapshot of the disease in 1998. Each year since, the United Nations has issued increasingly dire assessments: UNAIDS estimated that 36 million people around the world were infected in 2000, including 25 million in Africa. In 2002, the numbers were 42 million globally, with 29 million in Africa.

But by 2002, disparities were already emerging. A national study in the southern African country of Zambia, for example, found a rate of 15.6 percent, significantly lower than the U.N. rate of 21.5 percent. In Burundi, which borders Rwanda in central East Africa, a national study found a rate of 5.4 percent, not the 8.3 percent estimated by UNAIDS.

In West Africa, Sierra Leone, just then emerging from a devastating civil war, was found to have a national prevalence rate of less than 1 percent—compared with an estimated U.N. rate of 7 percent.

Such disparities, independent researchers say, skewed years of policy judgments and decisions on where to spend precious health-care dollars.

"From a research point of view, they've done a pathetic job," said Paul Bennell, a British economist whose studies of the impact of AIDS on African school systems have shown mortality far below what UNAIDS had predicted. "They were not predisposed, let's put it that way, to weigh the counterevidence. They were looking to generate big bucks."

The UN Must Revise Its Data

The United Nations started to revise its estimates in light of the new studies in its 2004 report, reducing the number of infections in Africa by 4.4 million, back to the total four years earlier of 25 million. It also gradually decreased the overall infection rate for working-age adults in sub-Saharan Africa, from 9 percent in a 2002 report to 7.2 percent in its report released in November 2005.

Peter Ghys, an epidemiologist who has worked for UNAIDS since 1999, acknowledged in an interview from his office in Geneva that HIV projections several years ago were too high because they relied on data from prenatal clinics.

But Ghys said the agency made the best estimates possible with the information available. As better data emerged, such as the new wave of national population studies, it has made revisions where necessary, he said.

"What has happened is we have come to realize that indeed we have overestimated the epidemic a bit," he said.

On its Web site, UNAIDS describes itself as "the chief advocate for worldwide action against AIDS." And many researchers say the United Nations' reliance on rigorous science waned after it created the separate AIDS agency in 1995—the first time the world body had taken this approach to tackle a single disease.

Questioning UNAIDS Motives

In the place of previous estimates provided by the World Health Organization, outside researchers say, the AIDS agency produced reports that increasingly were subject to political calculations, with the emphasis on raising awareness and money.

"It's pure advocacy, really," said Jim Chin, a former U.N. official who made some of the first global HIV prevalence estimates while working for WHO in the late 1980s and early 1990s. "Once you get a high number, it's really hard once the data comes in to say, 'Whoops! It's not 100,000. It's 60,000.'"

Chin, speaking from Stockton, Calif., added, "They keep cranking out numbers that, when I look at them, you can't defend them."

Ghys said he never sensed pressure to inflate HIV estimates. "I can't imagine why UNAIDS or WHO would want to do that," he said. "If we did that, it would just affect our credibility."

Ghys added that studies now show that the overall percentage of Africans with HIV has stabilized, though U.N. models still show increasing numbers of people with the virus because of burgeoning populations.

Many other researchers, including Wilson from the World Bank and two epidemiologists from the U.S. Agency for International Development who wrote a study published [in April 2006] in the *Lancet*, a British medical journal, dispute that conclusion, saying that the number of new cases in Africa peaked several years ago.

Some involved in the fight against AIDS say that tallying HIV cases is not nearly as important as finding the resources to fight the disease. That is especially true now that antiretroviral drugs are more affordable, making it possible to extend millions of lives if enough money and health-care workers are available to facilitate treatment.

"It doesn't matter how long the line is if you never get to the end of it," said Francois Venter, a South African doctor

The AIDS Epidemic Has Reached a Turning Point in Many African Countries

UNAIDS is mistaken to conclude so emphatically that HIV prevalence is not declining (and thus the epidemic has not reached a 'turning point') in a relatively large number of African countries.

Even UNAIDS's own national estimates show lower prevalence rates in 2003 in 20 out of the 24 higher-prevalence countries than two years earlier in 2001. While some of the lower figures for 2003 are due to better testing procedures rather than genuine declines in HIV prevalence, the much higher earlier estimates (in 1997, 1999, and 2001) in a significant number of countries shows the extent to which national prevalence rates have been overestimated. In overall terms, the UNAIDS estimate of HIV prevalence for sub-Saharan Africa as a whole has been lowered from 9.0 percent at the end of 2001 to 7.5 percent at the end of 2003.

Paul Bennell, "Is UNAIDS Right? Levels and Trends in HIV Prevalence in Sub-Saharan Africa," Eldis, 2004.

and head of Johannesburg General Hospital's rapidly expanding antiretroviral drug program, speaking in an interview in Johannesburg.

Bad Data May Hinder Effective Treatment

But to the researchers who drive AIDS policy, differences in infection rates are not merely academic. They scour the world looking for evidence of interventions that have worked, such as the rigorous enforcement of condom use at brothels in Thailand and aggressive public campaigns that have urged Ugandans to limit their sexual partners to one.

Programs deemed successful are urged on other countries and funded lavishly by international donors, often to the exclusion of other programs.

Rwanda, a mountainous country of about 8.5 million people jammed into a land area smaller than Maryland, has relied on approaches similar to those used in Uganda, and may have produced similar declines in HIV. UNAIDS estimated in 1998 that 370,000 Rwandans were infected, equal to 12.75 percent of all working-age adults and a substantial percentage of children as well. Every two years since, the agency has lowered that estimate—to 11.2 percent in 2000, 8.9 percent in 2002 and 5.1 percent in 2004.

Dirk van Hove, the top UNAIDS official in Rwanda, said the next official estimate, due in May [2006], would show an infection rate of "about 3 percent," in line with the new national study. He said the U.N. estimate tracked the declining prevalence.

Rwandan health officials say their national HIV infection rate might once have topped 3 percent and then declined. But it's just as likely, they say, that these apparent trends reflected nothing more than flawed studies.

Even so, Rwanda's cities show signs of a serious AIDS problem not yet tamed. The new study found that 8.6 percent of urban, working-age women have HIV. Overall, officials say, 150,000 Rwandans are infected, less than half the number estimated by UNAIDS in 1998.

Bruno Ngirabatware, a physician who has treated AIDS patients in Kigali since the 1980s, said he has seen no evidence of a recent decline in HIV infection rates.

"There's lots of patients there, always," he said.

> "HIV has increasingly become a disease of color, with blacks bearing the heaviest burden by far. African Americans make up just 13 percent of the U.S. population but account for an astounding 51 percent of new HIV diagnoses."

AIDS Is a Crisis in Black America

Claudia Kalb and Andrew Murr

In the following viewpoint, Claudia Kalb and Andrew Murr describe HIV/AIDS as one of the greatest crises in the African American community, where homophobia; distrust of the medical establishment; high rates of poverty, IV drug use, and STDs; and low levels of HIV testing all contribute to the spread of AIDS. Kalb and Murr applaud the efforts of young activists who run AIDS outreach and prevention programs in the absence of strong leadership in the black church. Claudia Kalb is a senior writer for Newsweek *magazine who writes primarily health stories. Andrew Murr, a correspondent in* Newsweek's *Los Angeles bureau, writes about science, medicine, and California politics.*

Claudia Kalb and Andrew Murr, "The Crisis in Black America," *MSNBC.com*, May 15, 2006. Republished with permission of MSNBC, conveyed through Copyright Clearance Center, Inc.

As you read, consider the following questions:

1. According to Kalb and Murr, what percentage of HIV infection in the black community occurs through heterosexual transmission and what percentage through homosexual transmission?

2. What is the "down-low" (DL) phenomenon, according to Kalb and Murr, and how does it contribute to the spread of HIV in the black community?

3. What attitudes in the black church work to hinder AIDS prevention, according to the authors?

It's a warm spring morning, and two dozen African-American women are gathered around a conference table at the Women's Collective in Washington, D.C. Easter is just a few days away, but nobody is thinking about painted eggs and bunny rabbits. The collective, less than two miles north of the White House, is a haven for HIV-positive women, and on this day the focus is on sex, condoms and prevention. "Our responsibility," says one woman in a rousing voice, "is to tell the truth!" Together, the women are on a mission to educate, empower themselves and stop the spread of the virus. Patricia Nalls, the collective's founder and executive director, asks the group to read a fact sheet about HIV and AIDS, a staggering array of statistics documenting the impact of the disease in the United States. "So now we know what's happening to us," says Nalls.

What's happening is an epidemic among black women, their husbands, boyfriends, brothers, sisters, sons and daughters. Twenty-five years after the virus was first documented in gay white men, HIV has increasingly become a disease of color, with blacks bearing the heaviest burden by far. African-Americans make up just 13 percent of the U.S. population but account for an astounding 51 percent of new HIV diagnoses. Black men are diagnosed at more than seven times the rate of white men, black females at 20 times the rate of white women.

Decades into the epidemic, scientists have made enormous strides in unlocking the disease at the molecular level. Understanding why HIV has taken hold of black America and how to prevent its spread has proved to be no less daunting a challenge. The root of the problem is poverty and the neglect that comes with it—inadequate health care and a dearth of information about safe sex. IV drug use, sexually transmitted diseases and high-risk sex (marked by multiple partners and no protection) have fueled transmission; homophobia and religious leaders steeped in moralistic doctrine have suppressed honest conversations about how to stop it. All the while, much of black leadership has been slow in responding, only recently mobilizing to protect its community. HIV, says Cathy Cohen, a political scientist at the University of Chicago and author of a book about blacks and AIDS, "is one of the greatest crises threatening the black community. It's the life and death of black people."

The crisis plays out in inner cities and rural towns alike, where money, education and access to good medical care are limited. Protecting against HIV isn't necessarily priority No. 1 among the poor. "If you're focused on day-to-day survival, you're not thinking about where to get condoms," says Marjorie Hill, of the Gay Men's Health Crisis in New York City. Alijah Burwell, 39, lives in a rundown 110-year-old clapboard house with seven family members in Oxford, N.C. Burwell, who was diagnosed with HIV eight years ago and has long had sex with both men and women, doesn't know which of his partners made him sick. "I had one too many" is all he'll say. But for several years after he was diagnosed, Burwell says, he continued to have sex, often unprotected. And he didn't tell the women that he was sleeping with men too. He also smoked crack and drank a lot. And though he sought treatment for HIV, he wasn't vigilant about taking his medication, spiking his viral load, which made him a greater threat to his partners.

Key Risk Factors: STDs and Lack of Testing

The virus once referred to as "gay-related immunodeficiency disease" has become increasingly gender-blind, especially in the black community, where heterosexual transmission accounts for 25 percent of male infections and 78 percent of female infections. Men who have sex with men still account for almost half of all male cases, and [in May 2006] the Centers for Disease Control and Prevention published data pinpointing two key risk factors for transmission: sexually transmitted diseases [STDs]—which facilitate infection—and low levels of testing among black men. STDs are a menace for both African-American men and women: gonorrhea rates, for example, are 26 times higher in black men than white men and 15 times higher in black females. Testing takes initiative, time and a willingness to overlook stigma on the part of both sexes.

Even 25 years on, that stigma is powerful. The AIDS and STD clinic in rural Henderson, N.C., is tucked away near the back of a one-story medical building. A small sign next to the door says NORTHERN OUTREACH CLINIC. Only inside, where HIV posters adorn the walls, is the clinic's mission clear. "No one wants anyone else to know they're infected," says Dr. Michelle Collins Ogle, who treats more than 200 men and women, mostly black and poor, ranging in age from 18 (a young woman who contracted HIV as a sexually active 10-year-old) to 79 (a widower who appears to have been infected by a young girl who traded sex for his financial support). Before funerals, family members will hint to Ogle that the presence of the woman known as "the AIDS doctor" would be embarrassing. Especially when they've told other loved ones that the cause of death was cancer.

Such denial is hardly uncommon. With powerful drugs saving lives, some African-Americans believe the threat is either over or limited to gay white men. Distrust of the medical establishment has never fully waned since the Tuskegee syphilis experiment, launched in the 1930s; in a 2005 poll, 27 per-

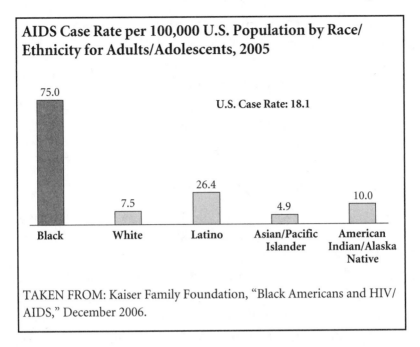

AIDS Case Rate per 100,000 U.S. Population by Race/ Ethnicity for Adults/Adolescents, 2005

75.0

U.S. Case Rate: 18.1

26.4

7.5

4.9

10.0

Black White Latino Asian/Pacific Islander American Indian/Alaska Native

TAKEN FROM: Kaiser Family Foundation, "Black Americans and HIV/ AIDS," December 2006.

cent of black Americans said they thought "AIDS was produced in a government laboratory." Every day, such wariness and misinformation breed new infections. In a recent five-city study of more than 2,000 gay and bisexual men, researchers found that nearly half of black men tested positive for HIV— and of those, an astounding two thirds did not know their status.

Burwell learned that he was positive after being tested while serving a drug sentence in prison—a hotbed for HIV, with a disproportionately high population of blacks. According to a new government study, the vast majority of HIV-positive inmates contract the virus before they enter prison. But some men become infected inside. Harold Atkins, 30, spent just over five years in San Quentin State Prison in California, where he was a peer educator for Centerforce, a group that provides HIV education to inmates. "There was a lot of sex happening in prison," says Atkins. There was not a lot of clarity about sexuality, however. "The same individual who had unprotected sex with males on the inside Monday through Friday would be in the visiting room with his wife and kids on Saturday and Sunday," says Atkins, who himself is HIV-negative. The men, who engaged in what Atkins calls "survival sex," did not consider themselves homosexual, and they didn't tell anybody on the outside what they were doing. "They'd say, 'I have sex with men. I'm not gay, they're gay.'"

Homophobia in the Black Community

Driving this sexual ambiguity is homophobia in the black community. The prototypical black male role model is big, strong and masculine; being gay or bisexual is weak. It's also a sin. "The church has caused people to go underground" about their sexuality, says the Rev. Charles Straight, who helped launch an AIDS ministry in 1984 and is now an assistant pastor at Wesley United Methodist Church in Chicago. "People are afraid to be who they are." That fear has driven some men to have sex with men "on the down-low" ["the DL"]: secretly indulging in homosexual behavior while keeping up the appearance of being straight—and sleeping with their girlfriends and wives without protection.

Is the DL contributing to the spread of HIV among blacks? There are no scientific data to support the hypothesis. And the phenomenon has caused consternation in the black community, where men already battle stereotypes about sexuality. But women who've fallen victim say people need to know that it happens. Margot, now 52, learned she was HIV-positive when she was pregnant in October 1991. Margot says she was never promiscuous and never used drugs. "My fault was that I slept with my husband," she says. Margot says her now ex-husband never discussed his sexuality, but through conversations with his family and her doctor, it became clear that he was having sex with a man, most likely a buddy from work. In January 1992, Margot's baby was born HIV-positive. In March

1994, she died. "It's so horrible," says Margot, "every day knowing you had to bury a child as a result of lies, mistrust and misdeeds."

The DL has made Oprah-esque headlines, but there are far less sinister factors involved in the spread of HIV. Dr. Donna Futterman, director of the Adolescent AIDS Program at the Children's Hospital at Montefiore Medical Center in the Bronx, N.Y., says about half of the young women she sees have had only one sex partner and don't consider themselves at risk. "They say, 'I can look into his eyes and know. He looks fine, he looks clean, he told me he loves me'," she says. Women, young and old, enter into or stay in risky relationships because they're desperate for financial security. They're also eager to be loved. Diane Campbell, 50, tested positive after she and her boyfriend stopped using condoms. Low self-esteem, says Campbell, played a major role: "I let my guard down with the wrong person." Women can infect men, too. Ricky Allen, 45, who is straight, believes he contracted HIV from his late wife, who infected their baby daughter. Both have since died.

Activists are determined to stop the dying, neighborhood by neighborhood. In Henderson, N.C., Ogle coordinates a team of outreach workers who preach safe sex and hand out condoms and dental dams, even in areas where crack is rampant and often traded for sex. Every week, the Center for Health Justice in Los Angeles distributes condoms to inmates in L.A. County jails, and at the Falkenberg Road Jail in Tampa, Fla., prisoners are given rapid HIV tests so they know their status before release. In New York, GMHC's Women's Institute sends Laverne Patent, a 54-year-old HIV-positive woman, to beauty salons; one recent Saturday morning, she gave out "pussy packs" containing condoms to clients at Hair Players 2000 in Brooklyn.

The Women's Collective, operating at an epicenter of the epidemic—the nation's capital has one of the highest rates of AIDS cases in the country—provides services and builds self-esteem even as it, and similar groups nationwide, battle debilitating cuts in funding. Black Entertainment Television, partnering with the Kaiser Family Foundation, spent $15 million in donated air time [in 2005] to run public-service announcements encouraging teens to "Rap It Up" and get tested—a potential inoculation against the nonstop bombardment of sexual music and videos. And the CDC, which devotes 43 percent of its $650 million HIV budget to the black community, is exploring new testing and prevention programs, like North Carolina's "d-Up," aimed at educating men at black bars and clubs, says Dr. Kevin Fenton, CDC's AIDS chief.

Nowhere is the need for change greater than in the black church. "It is the center of turning this crisis around," says Pernessa Seele, founder of the Balm in Gilead, which began mobilizing clergy in Harlem in 1989 and now works with 15,000 churches nationwide. The challenge is getting church leaders to acknowledge sexuality, not preach against it. "Too many pastors are still stuck on theological doctrine. They have not been able to see the suffering," says Seele. Progress is being made little by little. The Rev. Doris Green, of the AIDS Foundation of Chicago, has been pounding on pulpits for years. Some churches have shut their doors; others have braved the challenge. One even "did a condom demonstration in the church with a dildo!" says Green. "That blessed my heart."

The future of HIV in the black community is in the hands of young warriors like Marvelyn Brown and Shelton Jackson. Brown, who just turned 22, tested positive in 2003, the victim of unprotected sex with a guy she thought was her soulmate. News of her diagnosis "spread like death" in her hometown of Nashville, but Brown has refused to stay silent. She went public in a local paper in 2004 and is now working with Kaiser to get the message out. Last month Brown toured college campuses with Hope's Voice, a prevention outreach group aimed at young adults. At Brown University, after another speaker pointed out that kissing isn't a risk factor for HIV transmission, Brown quickly interjected: "It depends on what you kiss."

Jackson, 28 and HIV-positive, was on tour that day, too. An openly gay student at Morgan State University in Baltimore, Jackson watched his partner die of AIDS in 2002. Today, he's eager to break the stigma and dispel the myths. He says he'll talk to people about HIV "anywhere they will listen." His hope: if one man acts up, others may follow.

> *"There were well over 1 million cases of AIDS at the end of 2001 and . . . this number will most likely mushroom to 10 million by 2010."*

China Must Face the Possibility of an Explosive AIDS Epidemic

Richard Burger

In the following viewpoint, Richard Burger warns that the majority of China's 1.2 billion citizens have little knowledge of AIDS and little awareness that the main method of HIV transmission in China is through use of contaminated needles. About 70 percent of China's AIDS patients are from rural areas, where selling blood is a common way to earn extra money and where untested blood is mixed into the blood supply by unlicensed collection companies. Burger argues that social and political reluctance to discuss sex-related topics, or acknowledge problems such as prostitution or drug use for fear of embarrassment and stigmatization, means an explosive spread of HIV/AIDS in China is likely. Richard Burger is senior vice-president of the public relations agency Ketchum Newscan in Taipei and the author of the China-related blog The Peking Duck.

Richard Burger, "AIDS in China," *The Peking Duck*, April 14, 2003. http://peking duck.org. Reproduced by permission.

As you read, consider the following questions:

1. According to Burger, what regions of China have been hardest hit by the AIDS epidemic, and why?

2. What is wrong with the Chinese government's "Five-Year Plan of Action to Contain and Control HIV/AIDS," in the author's view?

3. How have restrictive laws and punitive measures exacerbated rather than curbed the AIDS epidemic in China, according to the author?

All indicators show that China is on the brink of an unprecedented explosion of the AIDS epidemic. Data prepared by UNAIDS, the Joint United Nation Programme on HIV/AIDS, indicate there were well over 1 million cases of AIDS at the end of 2001 and that this number will most likely mushroom to 10 million by 2010. About 70 percent of those infected are peasants living in rural areas.

Only in the mid-1990s did China start to acknowledge the worsening crisis, and the central government has been slow to take action. Currently only a few Chinese hospitals, all in the big coastal cities and far from the vast majority of infected citizens, are equipped to treat AIDS, and the cost of treatment is far too high for average citizens to afford. These factors, combined with the unwillingness of the government at the local level to take actions such as prevention awareness, converge to increase the likelihood of a future AIDS tragedy in China.

HIV Spread Mainly by Contaminated Needles

The main cause of AIDS in China has not been sexual transmission but contaminated needles, mainly those shared by injection drug users, but also needles used in unsanitary ways during paid plasma collection. In poorer parts of China, selling blood is a common way to earn extra money, especially for drug users and commercial sex workers. Tragically, many of the blood-collecting companies are unlicensed and illegal, and their use of contaminated needles has been a major factor in spreading the disease. Furthermore, those who sell blood to these companies are often in the most high-risk groups and have already been infected with HIV. Their blood is not tested, and is mixed into the blood pool and sold. Most of this occurs in poor, remote areas of China where there is less likely to be interference from authorities.

The epidemic is worse in provinces with a higher level of commercial sex and intravenous drug abuse. It is not surprising that the most severely affected area is along China's southwest territory, bordering "The Golden Triangle" along the Myanmar, Laos and Thai borders, a region famous for its heavy trade in heroin, methamphetamines and other illegal drugs. In the northwest province of Xinjiang there has also been a huge outbreak due to prostitution, sharing of needles for drug injection, and little to no awareness of AIDS and its prevention.

Cultural Taboos Block Treatment and Prevention Efforts

AIDS in China has been a taboo topic for years, and to a large extent it remains so today. This is key to understanding the evolution of the AIDS epidemic in China, and why confronting it is so challenging.

The Chinese culture and government tend to frown on sex education and to discourage open dialogue on controversial subjects like AIDS, which has made it difficult to raise awareness, especially in the rural parts of the country. Most Chinese citizens, especially in rural areas, are frightened to discuss sex-related topics, and have a hard time gathering the courage even to purchase condoms. Their local governing officials usually harbor the same fears. . . .

Both the central and provincial governments are highly reluctant to discuss anything that might reflect poorly on the

AIDS in China: Five Reasons for Concern

Several features of [China's AIDS] epidemic are already serious enough to cause grave concern. First, it [AIDS] has spread to every province and half the counties within them. Second, the number of reported cases is growing and, since 85% of those infected do not know they are HIV-positive, the growth will continue. Third, among certain groups, the infection is present in alarming proportions. Fourth, even a low prevalence rate, such as the World Health Organization's bottom-of-the-range 0.05%, means 650,000 infections; the government's rate translates into 840,000. Either means personal tragedy on a vast scale. This points to the fifth reason for concern: in a country as big as China, an AIDS explosion would have economic, political and social consequences for the entire world.

Economist, *"Anatomy of an Epidemic,"* July 28, 2005.

image of China, as this might have an adverse effect on tourism and/or foreign investment. Officially there is still no prostitution, no drug abuse, and no blood donation scandal in China.

While in recent years the central government has become more involved in raising awareness of AIDS and taking steps to prevent and contain it, the local and provincial governments have been slow to follow suit. Often they make the situation more difficult by refusing to acknowledge the AIDS crisis, as it might reflect poorly on them. It is at the local/ provincial level that most of China's 1.2 billion citizens deal with their government, and where they turn for help.

Because of the government's avoidance of the issue, the general public has little knowledge of AIDS and how it is affecting China. This in turn creates fear of AIDS patients, who are often fired from their jobs or banned from attending school. This contributes to a vicious circle, where the AIDS victims choose not to seek help for fear of losing their job or facing public disgrace.

Even [in 2003] AIDS has "no face" in China; it was only in 2001, at the Beijing International AIDS congress, that the first infected man was allowed to speak to a public audience. This was after the central government had implemented its "Five-year Plan of Action to Contain and Control of HIV/AIDS" with a set of specific goals for grappling with AIDS. Since that time, in 2002, there was actually a public wedding of an AIDS-infected couple, indicating a further shift toward coming to terms with the disease.

Inadequate Government Response

Still, the five-year plan continues to present AIDS strictly as a medical problem without considering the broader social-economic implications of the crisis. Thus, public awareness remains low. Some of the legislation has actually made the situation worse, especially at provincial and local levels. Many local governments simply do not want to know or let others know about AIDS in their respective regions, as it might make them look bad. So information is suppressed. In addition, local officials worry that an honest assessment of prostitution, illegal plasma collection and drug abuse in their region would lead to their being accused of incompetency.

Laws based on prejudice and fear exacerbate rather than curb the epidemic. Employers in Beijing, for example, are required to report "suspected AIDS patients" to local health authorities, reinforcing the notion that AIDS victims will be punished. In Hebei, all citizens with STDs are banned from entering school, getting married or working in service-related fields. Local and provincial laws are frequently in direct contradiction to national AIDS guidelines prepared by the central government's Ministry of Health.

International experience shows that restrictive laws and punitive measures have little effect in curbing AIDS, while there is no question that they can have a negative impact on both prevention and care. In a punitive environment, vulnerable people will be more inclined to avoid preventive outreach, and people will decline getting tested for HIV for fear of punishment and/or stigmatization.

"Silence Equals Death"

At the heart of the entire problem is awareness. When AIDS first surfaced in the US, the mantra for years was "Silence equals death." Sadly, that formula has proven to be totally correct when it comes to China. Keeping silent and ignoring the reality of AIDS has made the situation in China infinitely worse than it could/should have been.

Simply acknowledging the existence of these issues, let alone taking bold action on them, is challenging in a cultural environment that is inclined to minimize or ignore its problems, especially those related to traditionally "untouchable" topics like drugs, prostitution and homosexuality. Let us hope that the small steps China is only just beginning to take continue to accelerate, gathering increased momentum and determination. There is no time to waste.

> *"There is among international AIDS workers a sense that China is taking the epidemic seriously."*

China Is Confronting HIV/AIDS

Sabin Russell

After years of denying that it has an AIDS problem, China has acknowledged and is actively fighting its HIV/AIDS epidemic, Sabin Russell writes in the following viewpoint. Russell cites many-pronged treatment and prevention efforts established by the Chinese government, including clinics for IV drug users, condom distribution, free HIV testing, free antiviral drugs to rural residents with AIDS, new hospital AIDS wards, and needle-exchange programs. She also notes that UNAIDS has reduced its estimate of the number of Chinese living with HIV from 840,000 to 650,000, backing away from earlier dire predictions of an explosive rise in AIDS cases. Sabin Russell is the San Francisco Chronicle's *medical writer.*

Sabin Russell, "China Finally Taking Steps to Fight Its HIV Problem," *San Francisco Chronicle*, July 30, 2006, p. A17. Copyright © 2006 *San Francisco Chronicle*. Republished with permission of *San Francisco Chronicle*, conveyed through Copyright Clearance Center, Inc.

As you read, consider the following questions:

1. How did the outbreak of SARS in China in 2003 finally spur the Chinese government to respond vigorously to the HIV/AIDS epidemic, according to Russell?

2. What are the provisions of China's Four Frees and One Care Program?

3. According to the author, how does the contaminated-blood scandal in Henan province illustrate the Chinese government's inadequate response to HIV/AIDS in the mid-1990s *and* its improved response today?

A quarter-century into the global pandemic, the world's most populous nation has begun taking cautious steps to acknowledge the peril posed by HIV and to adopt some of the proven prevention and treatment programs of Western nations—such as methadone maintenance therapy—to control it.

An estimated 650,000 Chinese are living with HIV, a virus that has infiltrated the Middle Kingdom along ancient drug-trafficking routes and threatens to spread silently into a population that still deeply stigmatizes those who carry it.

Among those at high risk for AIDS are 120 million migrant workers, known as the *liudong renkou*, or floating population. Drawn from the impoverished rural areas where most of China's 1.3 billion people live today, they are a source of cheap labor powering this country's phenomenal economic expansion. Young, single and mostly male, they live in single-sex dormitories and have ready access to drugs and prostitutes.

They also fall through the widening cracks in China's public health infrastructure. Scenarios like these have fueled the epidemic in Africa and India and could threaten this nation's push toward prosperity.

In 1998, China's Ministry of Health forecast that, absent a vigorous program of prevention and treatment, 10 million of its citizens could be living with HIV infection by 2010. Outside forecasters, such as the Center for Strategic and International Studies in Washington, warned of twice as many infections in the same time frame.

China has recently backed away from such dire predictions—the [2006] report written by the Chinese government and UNAIDS, the Joint United Nations Programme on HIV/AIDS, makes no estimate of future infections. Citing more accurate surveys, it lowered from 840,000 to 650,000—a drop of 23 percent—its estimate of the number of people in China living with HIV.

The new number may, in fact, be a more accurate representation of the epidemic's toll in China, but surveillance remains uneven, and testing is inadequate. By the official count, there were 70,000 new HIV infections in China [in 2005] and 25,000 deaths from AIDS. Nearly 80 percent of those living with HIV in the country do not know it. By comparison, only about 25 percent of Americans with HIV are unaware of their infection.

In Changsha, a city of nearly 1.5 million, public health leaders and Communist Party government officials have put together a package of prevention measures ranging from condom distribution to HIV testing centers to new methadone-treatment clinics.

Targeting Drug Use

Heroin is a significant problem for China, and injection drug use is linked to 45 percent of the country's HIV cases. Hunan province is one of seven in China where more than 10,000 drug users are infected. . . .

Tianxin district authorities opened [its] methadone clinic before a crowd of local television reporters in February [2006] and have been carefully tracking its progress since. By the end of May [2006], 72 addicts had entered the program—the goal is to enroll 200.

There have been setbacks. Eight participants have been thrown out after urine tests showed they were still using heroin—not uncommon in methadone programs worldwide. More troublesome was a police sweep of addicts in April. Clinic officials say the raid was incorrectly rumored in the community to be linked to participation in the methadone program. The result was that new monthly enrollments dropped from 38 to 18.

Zhiyong Fu, director of the Tianxin district Center for Disease Control, said the health department is working with police to reduce tensions between public security authorities and drug users who want to participate in the methadone program. He said there are also plans to relax the requirement that addicts first stay in a rehabilitation center before coming to the clinic, so more of them will sign up.

Targeting Prostitution

Changsha's HIV-prevention efforts also focus on the nighttime entertainment industry that is burgeoning in the new China. UNAIDS estimates that there are 127,000 prostitutes in China living with HIV—about 20 percent of all cases in the country.

Across town in the Furong district, Changsha's deputy mayor Dr. Cao Ya—a Xiangya School of Medicine professor who spent several years at the National Cancer Institute in Maryland—led visitors through the Wan Bao hotel. Here, condoms are distributed in guest rooms and at popular karaoke salons.

"The central government has stipulated that all public entertainment places have to have condoms," she explained.

[In 2005] 40 hotels in the Furong district began offering condoms in a pilot program. Now, she said, all the hotels there are complying with the new policy. With government subsidies, condoms distributed through the program are either free or are sold for as little as 10 cents each.

Failure to provide condoms can, in theory, lead to fines of up to $600, but Changsha public health administrator Peng Hongei said the emphasis today is not on punishment, but persuasion. "It's a process," he said. "At first, we stress self-compliance."

Expanding Medical Treatment

In Beijing, 850 miles to the north, construction workers are busily adding a four-story addition to the You An Hospital, one of only two medical centers in China that specialize in AIDS. It has a 20-bed ward offering care to seriously ill AIDS patients. The new project will expand its capacity tenfold.

The need for specialty hospitals is apparent. "Stigma is a massive issue. Most doctors won't touch you if you have HIV," said Drew Thompson, National Director of the China-MSD Partnership in Beijing, a joint project between the Chinese Health ministry and pharmaceutical company Merck.

A center for treatment of infectious diseases, You An Hospital was a focal point during the 2003 SARS outbreak—an occurrence that many health officials in China credit with bringing the country out of isolation on medical matters. Initial efforts to hide the extent of SARS in Beijing eventually led to the sacking of the mayor and China's health minister, but the central government now considers its resolution of that crisis as a success story and a model for openness about such matters in the future.

"SARS loosened them up. They found they could reveal a vulnerability and not get criticized for it," said Dr. Eric Goosby, president of the Pangea Foundation in San Francisco.

Another event often credited with spurring China's leaders on AIDS was a visit by former President Bill Clinton and his public embrace of 21-year-old HIV-positive activist Song Pengfei during a news conference in Beijing in November 2003. . . .

China Is Joining the Global Fight Against AIDS

China learned a hard lesson from the SARS epidemic in 2003: that it cannot keep infectious diseases—SARS, AIDS or bird flu—a state secret.

"I think China is trying very hard to play the good global citizen; that it's really about the geo-politics of infectious diseases and also relations within East Asia," said Dr. Gabriel Leung of the University of Hong Kong. "The Chinese leadership truly wants to have a very strong handle on infectious diseases—not just on pandemic influenza—but also on HIV/AIDS."

Charles Hadlock, "China Making Moves to Stem the Tide of AIDS,"
NBC News, December 2, 2005.

The next month, Chinese Premier Wen Jiabao and Vice Premier Wu Yi were seen for the first time shaking hands of hospitalized AIDS patients in front of national news media.

The Four Frees and One Care Program

China subsequently announced its Four Frees and One Care program. It offers free HIV testing; free antiviral drugs to rural residents with AIDS; free drugs to [HIV-infected] pregnant women; free schooling for AIDS orphans; and economic assistance to people living with the disease.

Whether the Chinese commitment runs deeper than showcase pilot programs and sloganeering remains to be seen. UNAIDS points out that implementation of the Four Frees program has been "relatively poor" in some regions. Nevertheless, there is among international AIDS workers a sense that China is taking the epidemic seriously.

Goosby, who works with the Clinton Foundation on Chinese AIDS projects, said a 3-year-old Pangea program in Yunnan province has become a model of the continuum of care needed to treat a drug-related HIV epidemic. In a province that borders the opium-growing regions of Burma and is burdened with heavy injection-drug use, the program provides needle exchange for addicts, methadone for those who want it and antiviral treatment for at least some of those who have AIDS.

It's just one more sign of measurable progress in China's newly invigorated fight against HIV. There are now 91 needle exchange programs and 128 methadone clinics nationwide. Central government spending has risen to $100 million from $12 million in 2001. But of the 75,000 officially recognized AIDS cases, only 20,000 are receiving AIDS drugs.

China's most unique HIV problem is a cohort of villagers in Henan province who became infected in the early 1990s through the unscrupulous practices of commercial blood sellers—clinics that paid donors for plasma. They separated red blood cells from the plasma, and then reinfused the donors with pooled red blood cells so they could donate more frequently. But the pooled blood was contaminated with HIV, and estimates are that 70,000 to 250,000 villagers became infected as a consequence.

Henan province's roughshod treatment of Chinese reporters who broke the story of the infected-blood sellers is a cautionary tale and reminder that this fast-growing nation remains a police state. At the provincial level, there remains an aversion to bad press and media crusades for government accountability. AIDS activists and whistle-blowers have reason to fear. In 2002, Beijing activist Dr. Wan Yanhai was jailed for 27 days because he published on his Web site a Henan provincial government document about the HIV outbreak there. He had earlier infuriated authorities there by publicly naming government officials who allegedly were complicit in the blood-selling scheme.

Yet the international scolding endured by China for jailing Wan may have contributed to its improved response to AIDS. In March 2003, China launched a program to provide AIDS drugs to the infected blood donors in Henan. Although there were problems with drug quality at the start, it was the first step toward provision of antiviral medicines to infected patients throughout the country.

Boosting Antiviral Drug Production

Although China has only begun to roll out antiviral drugs for its HIV cases, the country has already become one of the major suppliers of the raw materials used in AIDS drugs throughout the world.

[In 2005] Xiamen Mchem Pharma Group of Xiamen cut a deal with the William Jefferson Clinton Foundation to supply raw materials for AIDS drugs for sale in 40 poor countries. The company provides the chemicals to major generic AIDS drugmakers in India such as Cipla, Hetero and Ranbaxy. The firm said it can produce enough antiviral drugs to treat 400,000 people, and can sell the active ingredient for AZT for 20 percent below the international wholesale price.

Desano, a 10-year-old vitamin and drug manufacturer in Shanghai, currently makes the active ingredients for 14 antiviral drugs. It is a major supplier to generic drugmakers in India, Brazil and Thailand. Since 2002, it has been producing generic drugs for the domestic market, where it now sells its own versions of the antivirals ddI, AZT, nevirapine and d4T.

The new drug companies are typical of China's new entrepreneurial bent: fast-growing, high tech and global in their reach. Whether China will invest that sort of energy and expertise to deal with its own AIDS problem remains to be seen, but the future course of the epidemic, and the fate of millions, may turn on the answer.

Periodical Bibliography

The following articles have been selected to supplement the diverse views presented in this chapter.

Lawrence K. Altman	"Scientists Urge New Look At Feeding in AIDS Fight," *New York Times*, February 27, 2007.
Lawrence K. Altman	"AIDS Is on the Rise Worldwide, U.N. Finds," *New York Times*, November 22, 2006.
Hazel Barrett	"Too Little, Too Late: Response to the HIV/ AIDS Epidemics in Sub-Saharan Africa," *Geography*, Summer 2007.
Clark Champ	"Save Africa's Kids Now," *People*, December 5, 2005.
Christianity Today	"The AIDS Team," August 2006.
Paul de Lay, Robert Greener, and Jose Antonio Izazola	"Are We Spending Too Much on HIV? NO," *British Medical Journal*, February 17, 2007.
Danny Dorling, Mary Shaw, and George Davey Smith	"Global Inequality of Life Expectancy Due to AIDS," *British Medical Journal*, March 18, 2006.
Beverley Haddad	"Reflections on the Church and HIV/AIDS," *Theology Today*, April 2005.
Denise B. Hawkins	"The Face of AIDS: Overwhelmingly Black and Female," *Diverse: Issues in Higher Education*, September 21, 2006.
Mark W. Kline	"Perspectives on the Pediatric HIV/AIDS Pandemic: Catalyzing Access of Children to Care and Treatment," April 2006.
MMWR: Morbidity & Mortality Weekly Report	"The Global HIV/AIDS Pandemic, 2006," August 11, 2006.
Society	"Child Deaths Due to AIDS," September–October 2005.

OPPOSING
VIEWPOINTS®
SERIES

CHAPTER 2

What Causes AIDS?

Chapter Preface

Accusing People of Causing AIDS

The debate over what causes AIDS can be contentious. Tensions around the topic only increase when groups of people are blamed for causing or spreading HIV infection. Assigning shame and disgrace to victims of an illness has been a common reaction to disease throughout history. Other maladies that have carried considerable stigma include leprosy, tuberculosis, cancer, mental illness, and many sexually transmitted diseases (STDs). AIDS is only the latest illness to be stigmatized, and the severity of the stigma has prompted a special area of research to combat the detrimental consequences of blaming people for AIDS. During the AIDS epidemic, the targets of often misguided rejection, condemnation, and even violence have included gay men, Africans, and Haitians.

Since many of the first people with AIDS to be diagnosed by the medical establishment were gay men in the United States, AIDS was—and sometimes still is—assumed to be a gay illness. As knowledge about the syndrome grew, it became clear that HIV does not discriminate: Anyone who engages in certain unsafe behaviors, such as unprotected sexual contact and IV needle sharing, is at risk of being infected with HIV. Nevertheless, the fear of AIDS is sometimes exacerbated by anti-gay sentiment, as in the case of New York's Rabbi Yehuda Levin who speculated that AIDS "is a physical reflection of God's displeasure with this kind of biological misbehavior [gay relationships]." Similarly, the televangelist Reverend Jerry Falwell stated that "AIDS is not just God's punishment for homosexuals; it is God's punishment for the society that tolerates homosexuals." In addition to hostility, stigmatizing people who suffer from a disease can lead to denial or indifference. Many in the gay and lesbian community argue that the U.S.

government's slow initial response to the AIDS epidemic was due to the sexual orientation of the early victims. They say that because they were gay, few politicians cared enough to mobilize funding and research.

On the other hand, when Western scientists attributed AIDS to a simian form of the virus that jumped from African green monkeys to humans in Africa, this origin story of AIDS placed Africa in a bad light. Anti-AIDS sentiment gave way to the political scapegoating of Africans. In reaction, several African governments refused to share the incident rates of AIDS in their countries out of fear of losing foreign investments and tourism. Yet another scientific theory speculated that HIV came to North America through Haiti, leading some Americans to blame Haitians for causing AIDS. In a sensational controversy in 1992, 140 Haitian refugees were denied admission to the United States on the basis of being HIV positive. Their long detention in quarantine centers at Guantanamo Bay raised accusations of human rights violations. During the controversy, Haitians already living in the United States suffered from being associated with AIDS. Some lost jobs, housing, and educational opportunities because they were perceived to be "high risk" whether or not they were HIV positive.

Those who study the stigmatization of people with AIDS caution that it can harm the general public just as much as it harms the victims of stigma. Shame and ostracism associated with a disease can undermine public health efforts, making it all the more difficult to combat the epidemic. Researchers have found that fear of being stigmatized discourages people from being tested for HIV, from using prophylactics such as condoms to make sexual relations safer, and from getting medical care if they test positive. Since these risky behaviors can worsen the epidemic, intervention programs often include educational initiatives to reduce the stigma of AIDS along with their prevention and treatment plans.

| *"The evidence [that HIV causes AIDS] is now strong enough to put the case beyond all reasonable doubt."*

HIV Causes AIDS

Rob Noble

In the following viewpoint, Rob Noble argues that the retrovirus HIV causes AIDS because it satisfies all four of Koch's postulates, the four conditions historically accepted by scientists and doctors as sufficient proof that a particular germ causes a particular disease. Noble backs up his claim with evidence from the U.S. Centers for Disease Control and Prevention, the National Institutes of Health, and research studies from 1983 to 2004, a cumulative record that he maintains no dissident theorists have been able to disprove. Rob Noble is a spokesperson for AVERT, an international AIDS charity based in the United Kingdom, dedicated to public education and prevention of HIV/AIDS.

As you read, consider the following questions:

1. According to Noble, how does HIV satisfy Koch 1 even though many people are diagnosed with AIDS without being tested for HIV?

2. The dissident Perth Group claims that HIV has never been properly isolated and therefore has never been proven to exist. According to the author, by this unreasonable standard, what other viruses have never been proven to exist?

3. How does HIV satisfy Koch 3 (the germ must cause the disease when introduced into a healthy person) when no such experiment could ethically take place?

In the nineteenth century, the German scientist Robert Koch developed a set of four "postulates" to guide people trying to prove that a germ causes a disease. Scientists agree that if HIV satisfies all of these conditions with regard to AIDS then it must be the cause of AIDS:

- Koch 1: The germ must be found in every person with the disease

- Koch 2: The germ must be isolated from someone who has the disease and grown in pure culture

- Koch 3: The germ must cause the disease when introduced into a healthy person

- Koch 4: The germ must be re-isolated from the infected person . . .

Koch 1 Test

The U.S. Centers for Disease Control and Prevention (CDC) defines a condition called idiopathic CD4+ T-lymphocytopenia, or ICL for short. Someone is diagnosed with ICL if they have a CD4+ cell count below 300 cells per cubic millimeter, or 20% of all T lymphocytes, on at least two occasions, but have no detectable HIV infection, nor any other known cause of immune deficiency (such as cancer therapy). As many dissidents have pointed out, this is essentially a definition of HIV-free AIDS. So just how common is this condition?

In 1993, a CDC task force published the results of an exhaustive survey of ICL in the USA. They had reviewed 230,179 AIDS-like cases reported since 1983 and identified 47 patients with ICL (plus 127 uncertain cases). All of the other people with AIDS who had received an HIV test produced a positive result. What's more, the team closely investigated the ICL cases and discovered that they didn't fit the usual AIDS profile. There were 29 male and 18 female patients, and 39 of them were white (4 others were of Asian descent). In 29 cases, the researchers couldn't fit the people into conventional risk groups for AIDS (homosexual men, haemophiliacs, injecting drug users, and the sexual partners of such groups). Whatever these 47 cases represent, they don't seem to be typical of the massive epidemic that we're interested in.

The findings of the ICL survey are backed up by large-scale monitoring studies, including the Multicenter AIDS Cohort Study (MACS). During the MACS, scientists monitored the health of 2,713 gay and bisexual men who tested negative for HIV antibodies. Over several years, only one of these men had persistently low CD4+ cell counts, and he was undergoing cancer therapy designed to weaken his immune system. Similar results have been found among blood donors, recipients of blood and blood products, injecting drug users and other groups: severe immune deficiency is virtually non-existent among those who test HIV-negative.

As [AIDS dissident Peter] Duesberg has pointed out, quite a lot of people (mostly in the early 1980s) have been diagnosed with AIDS in the USA despite never taking an HIV test, and nobody knows whether these people were HIV-positive or not. However, based on the much larger sample of people who *have* been tested, Koch's first postulate has certainly been satisfied. The only way by which dissidents have been able to come up with significant numbers of HIV-free "AIDS" cases is by using much looser definitions of AIDS. Such definitions include many people with milder immune deficiency, which is generally not fatal.

What About False Positive Test Results?

Diagnosis of infection using antibody testing is one of the best-established concepts in medicine. The World Health Organisation and the U.S. National Institutes of Health agree that modern HIV tests are extremely reliable, and are even more accurate than most other infectious disease tests.

Nevertheless, some dissidents have tried to dismiss the association between AIDS and HIV by claiming that many of those who test positive are not really infected with HIV. In particular, Christine Johnson has listed dozens of conditions reported to have produced false positive reactions on at least one occasion (under particular circumstances, using particular test kits).

It is true that no test is perfect. However, what the dissidents usually don't mention is how rare the reports of false positive results have been, especially in recent years. Nor do they mention that every person who uses a test kit is trained to spot the telltale signs of a suspicious result, and to keep testing by various methods until no doubt remains. The conditions that cause false positive results are not only very uncommon, but are also typically short-lived, whereas HIV infection does not go away.

The dissident theory cannot satisfactorily explain why scientists have been able to use various techniques to detect the virus itself in virtually everyone with AIDS, as well as in most people with positive antibody test results. . . . These methods (including DNA PCR, RNA PCR and viral culture) are not affected by any of the factors said to produce false positive results in antibody testing.

Nor can the alternative theory fully explain why the association between AIDS and antibody test results is so exceptionally strong: virtually everyone with AIDS tests positive, while more than 99% of the U.S. public tests negative. And it cannot explain why the proportion of people testing HIV positive should have increased so dramatically over time. For example, the proportion of South African women testing HIV positive in annual antenatal surveys rose from 0.8% in 1990 to 10.4% in 1995, 24.5% in 2000 and 29.5% in 2004. The age distribution of these data is similar to that of other sexually transmittted infections.

Koch 2 Test

Koch required that the germ be isolated from all other material that could possibly cause disease, so that his third and fourth postulates could be properly tested.

In May 1983, Luc Montagnier and his colleagues in France reported the isolation of a virus they named LAV, which infected and killed CD4+ cells. A year later, the American Robert Gallo announced he had isolated a virus called HTLV-III and found a way to grow it in culture. It was later discovered that the two viruses were genetically indistinguishable, and they were renamed HIV.

Researchers have been able to isolate and culture HIV from most AIDS patients whom they have examined (as well as from many other people with HIV antibodies). They have isolated the virus from blood cells, blood plasma, lymph nodes, semen, vaginal fluids, amniotic fluids, bone marrow, brain, cerebrospinal fluid, intestines, breast milk, saliva, urine and tears, and cultured, it in various cell types. Images taken using electron microscopy and other techniques have shown virus-like particles that have the size, shape, structure, density, proteins and behaviour expected of retroviruses.

Techniques developed in the mid-1990s have made it much easier to extract and sequence the complete genetic material (genome) of an isolated virus. The Los Alamos database now contains hundreds of full-length HIV genomes from around the world, each containing the same nine genes. Based on genetic similarities and differences, these sequences have been used to define family trees of HIV types, groups and subtypes as well as hybrids called recombinant forms.

Only HIV Predicts AIDS

- Street drugs cannot be the cause of AIDS: A U.S. study found that people who used cocaine, heroin, dagga [an African folk name for cannabis] and poppers did not develop AIDS unless they were HIV-positive.

- Laboratory workers who contracted HIV have developed AIDS. No other proposed causes of AIDS were applicable to them.

- A Canadian study followed more than 700 gay men for eight years. Only those that contracted HIV developed AIDS.

- Malnutrition and poverty cannot be the cause of AIDS, although they do speed up the time that people with HIV develop AIDS or die. Not a single study has shown that AIDS develops in poor people who do not have HIV. Many well-off people have died of AIDS. One Ugandan study actually showed that poverty is not the cause of AIDS: it found a higher death-rate from AIDS among civil servants and well-educated people.

- Studies among people who receive blood transfusions, children and sex workers have also shown that only having HIV predicts AIDS.

- Studies also show that people with more HIV in their bodies are more likely to have AIDS.

Nathan Geffen, "How We Know That HIV Causes AIDS,"
Equal Treatment, *Treatment Action Campaign, March 2006.*

Whole or partial HIV genomes have been detected in numerous AIDS patients, using a technique called PCR (the same technology is used to find DNA evidence with which to convict murderers or to settle paternity suits, as well as to detect the germs that cause hepatitis, tuberculosis and other diseases). Almost everyone who tests positive for HIV genetic material also tests positive for HIV antibodies, and vice versa, while those who test negative for one thing also lack the other. People who have been exposed to the same source of infection contain genetically very similar HIV strains—similar enough for court convictions.

Scientists have used a standard technique of genetic science called molecular cloning to obtain highly purified HIV. Genetic material extracted using PCR or other techniques has been introduced into bacteria or other cells (usually using phages or plasmids), which then produce many exact copies (clones) of the viral genes. If cloned viral genomes are inserted (transfected) into human cells then they produce a new generation of infectious HIV particles, which are free from contamination.

Virtually all experts agree that HIV has been isolated according to the most rigorous standards of modern virology, meaning that Koch's second postulate has without doubt been satisfied.

What About the Perth Group?

A small band of Australian scientists and physicians claims that HIV has never been properly isolated. The Perth Group has never said that HIV doesn't exist; rather they say that HIV has never been conclusively proven to exist. They don't trust any HIV tests, because they have not been verified using their "gold standard" of isolated virus. The Group uses the isolation argument to dismiss just about every type of evidence that HIV causes AIDS.

Virtually all virologists believe that the Perth Group's conditions are unnecessary. They say nobody has ever used such rules to isolate any type of virus, and that other techniques are much more effective. According to the Perth Group's rules, nobody has isolated or proven the existence of the viruses said to cause small pox, influenza, measles, mumps and yellow fever.

Experts argue that the Group's rules are unreasonably demanding and impossible to satisfy fully, even though their main requirements have already been met. Dr. Duesberg is among those who have tried in vain to persuade the Perth Group that HIV definitely exists and has been isolated using the most rigorous methods available. None of the Perth Group has any qualifications in virology or AIDS research.

Koch 3 and 4 Test

The third and fourth postulates are much harder to prove. It's considered unethical to deliberately infect someone with pure HIV, so such an experiment has never taken place. However, there is no reason why the transmission has to be deliberate.

There have been three reports of lab workers developing immune deficiency after accidentally exposing themselves to purified, cloned HIV. As mentioned above, such cloned virus is free of all contamination from the original source. None of these people fitted conventional risk groups for the disease. In each case, HIV was isolated from the individual and, by genetic sequencing, was found to be the strain to which they'd been exposed. One of these workers developed PCP and had a CD4+ cell count below 50 cells before starting antiretroviral treatment.

Still, three examples don't make a totally conclusive proof, so it's worth looking for more evidence.

One line of argument can be based on animal experiments. In some studies, chimpanzees deliberately infected with HIV-1 have gone on to develop AIDS-like conditions (though this appears to be rare), while HIV-2 has had the same effect on baboons. Macaque monkeys have developed AIDS after being infected with a hybrid virus called SHIV, which contains genes taken from HIV. And in mice engineered to have a human immune system, HIV produces the same patterns of disease as in humans.

If we're prepared to bend the rules a bit further, we can look at people who've been infected with non-purified HIV. Such cases at least suggest that AIDS is infectious, though they don't rule out the possibility that more than one germ is involved.

Scientists have documented numerous cases of people developing AIDS after becoming infected with HIV as a result of blood transfusions, drug use, mother-to-child transmission, occupational exposure and sexual transmission. In such cases, they have recorded the development of HIV antibodies (seroconversion) using a series of blood tests, before progression to AIDS. Seroconversion is often accompanied by a mild flu-like illness or swollen glands.

Until the mid-1990s, nobody claimed that HIV had fulfilled Koch's last two postulates. Even today, the proof is not quite perfect. But most scientists believe the evidence is now strong enough to put the case beyond all reasonable doubt.

"All the epidemiological and microbiological evidence taken together conclusively demonstrates that HIV cannot cause AIDS or any other illness."

HIV Does Not Cause AIDS

Christine Maggiore

Christine Maggiore was diagnosed HIV-positive in 1992. She refused antiretroviral drugs and other standard AIDS therapies and became an active supporter of the dissident theory that HIV does not cause AIDS. She maintains that she remains in excellent health, and that the 2005 death of her three-year-old daughter was caused by an allergic reaction to antibiotics, not (as doctors concluded) to AIDS-related pneumonia. Maggiore is the founder of Alive & Well, an organization that questions common assumptions about AIDS and promotes alternative medical choices for HIV-positive people. In the following viewpoint, Maggiore challenges what she calls the HIV hypothesis.

As you read, consider the following questions:

1. In Maggiore's view, why did AIDS researchers rush to advance the hypothesis that HIV causes AIDS in the 1980s?

Christine Maggiore, "Is HIV the Cause of AIDS?" *Alive and Well: AIDS Alternatives*, 2004. http://aliveandwell.org. Reproduced by permission of Alive & Well AIDS Alternatives.

2. What evidence does the author present that retroviruses such as HIV are not toxic?

3. According to Maggiore, how do claims that HIV has a long latency period actually indicate that it does not cause AIDS?

There is no proof that HIV causes AIDS. In fact, all the epidemiological and microbiological evidence taken together conclusively demonstrates that HIV cannot cause AIDS or any other illness. The concept that AIDS is caused by a virus is not a fact, but a belief that was introduced at a 1984 press conference by Dr. Robert Gallo, a researcher employed by the National Institutes of Health (NIH).

HIV is a retrovirus, a type of virus studied meticulously during two decades of federal health programs that centered around the search for a cancer virus. The idea of contagious cancer was a popular notion in the 1960s and 70s. Since retroviruses have no cell-killing mechanisms, and cancer is a condition marked by rapid cell growth, this type of virus was considered a viable candidate for the cause of cancer. However, healthy people live in harmony with an uncountable number of harmless retroviruses; some are infectious while others are endogenous, produced by our own DNA. Few, if any, retroviruses have been shown to cause disease in humans.

AIDS Researchers' Questionable Motives

In the 1980s when the CDC began to direct its attention to AIDS, Gallo and other cancer researchers switched their focus from cancer to the newly identified dilemma called AIDS, and the same government scientists who led the quest for a cancer virus began to search for a virus that could cause AIDS.

On April 23, 1984, Gallo called an international press conference in conjunction with the US Department of Health and Human Services (HHS). He used this forum to announce his discovery of a new retrovirus described as "the probable cause of AIDS." Although Gallo presented no evidence to support his tentative assumption, the HHS immediately characterized it as "another miracle of American medicine ... the triumph of science over a dreaded disease."

Later that same day, Gallo filed a patent for the antibody test now known as the "AIDS test." By the following day, the *New York Times* had turned Gallo's proposal into a certainty with front page news of "the virus that causes AIDS," and all funding for research into other possible causes of AIDS came to an abrupt halt.

By announcing his hypothesis to the media without providing substantiating data, Gallo violated a fundamental rule of the scientific process. Researchers must first publish evidence for a hypothesis in a medical or scientific journal, and document the research or experiments that were used to construct it. Experts then examine and debate the hypothesis, and attempt to duplicate the original experiments to confirm or refute the original findings. Any new hypothesis must stand up to the scrutiny of peer review and must be verified by successful experiments before it can be considered a reasonable theory.

In the case of HIV, Gallo announced an unconfirmed hypothesis to the media who reported his idea as if it were an established fact, inciting government officials to launch new public health policies based on the unsubstantiated notion of an AIDS virus. Some attribute these violations of the scientific process to the atmosphere of terror and desperation that surrounded the notion of an infectious epidemic.

The data Gallo used to construct his HIV/AIDS hypothesis were published several days after his announcement. Rather than supporting his hypothesis, this paper revealed that Gallo was unable to find HIV (actual virus) in more than half of the AIDS patients in his study. While he was able to detect antibodies in most, antibodies alone are not an indication of current infection and are actually an indication of immunity from infection.

His paper also failed to provide a credible explanation as to how a retrovirus could cause AIDS. Gallo suggested that HIV worked by destroying immune cells, but 70 years of medical research had shown that retroviruses are unable to kill cells, and he offered no proof that HIV differed from other harmless retroviruses. In fact, all evidence to date conclusively demonstrates that HIV—like all retroviruses—is not cytotoxic [producing a toxic effect on cells].

The focus of questions about HIV quickly shifted from how it could cause AIDS to who found the now valuable viral commodity after Dr. Luc Montagnier of the Pasteur Institute in France accused Gallo of stealing his HIV sample. A congressional investigation determined that Gallo had presented fraudulent data in his original paper on HIV, and that the virus he claimed to have discovered had been sent to him by Montagnier. Negotiations were conducted between the French and American governments to establish discovery and patent rights. These ended in a compromise, with Montagnier and Gallo sharing credit as the codiscoverers of HIV and ownership rights to the HIV test. Montagnier has since stated that he does not believe HIV alone is capable of causing AIDS.

Retroviruses Are Not Toxic

Since 1984, more than 100,000 papers have been published on HIV. None of these papers, singly or collectively, has been able to reasonably demonstrate or effectively prove that HIV causes AIDS. Although Gallo claimed that HIV caused AIDS by destroying the T cells of the immune system, 20 years of cancer research confirmed that retroviruses are not cytotoxic. In fact, there is still no evidence in the scientific literature demonstrating that HIV is able to destroy T cells, directly or indirectly.

HIV May Not Even Exist

If HIV were the cause of "AIDS," or any other form of illness, then there would be HIV infection in every case of the disease. This is the logic of Koch's First Postulate, a standard test of whether an infectious agent causes a disease. Not only does HIV flunk Koch's First Postulate, it has never been properly isolated. Although we all have seen pictures of HIV, these are merely artists' renditions of what HIV is assumed to look like. In reality, it has never been seen through the electron microscope, and may not even exist in a cell-free, infectious form.

John Lauritzen, "AIDS: A Death Cult,"
Gay and Lesbian Humanist, *Winter 2003–2004.*

Comparing HIV to Varicella Zoster Virus (VZV), the known cause of chicken pox, highlights some of the ways in which HIV defies rules of science and logic.

HIV is the only virus that is said to cause a group of diseases caused by other viruses and bacteria rather than causing its own disease. AIDS experts also say that HIV is able to cause cell depletion—loss of immune cells—at the same time it causes cell proliferation or cancer.

Although more research money has been spent on HIV than on the combined total of all other viruses studied in medical history, there is no scientific evidence validating the hypothesis that HIV is the cause of AIDS, or that AIDS has a viral cause. A good hypothesis is defined by its ability to solve problems and mysteries, make accurate predictions and produce results. The HIV hypothesis has failed to meet any of these criteria. Hundreds of scientists around the world are now requesting an official reevaluation of the HIV hypothesis. . . .

Is the Rate of HIV Increasing?

HIV is not on the rise. According to the most recent CDC estimates, the number of HIV positive Americans has not increased once since the HIV test was introduced into general use in 1985.

In 1986, the CDC began promoting the estimate that 1 million to 1.5 million Americans were HIV positive. Media and AIDS organizations employed this figure to make the disturbing claim that one in every 250 people in the nation was infected with HIV. Four years later, official estimates were lowered to between 800,000 and 1.2 million, and in 1995, following an investigation by *NBC Nightly News*, the CDC again decreased their official estimate to between 650,000 and 900,000, a figure still promoted today [in 2004].

While the number of HIV positives has failed to grow, it is important to note that rates of venereal diseases such as chlamydia, genital herpes, gonorrhea and syphilis have increased throughout most of the AIDS epidemic and far surpass cases of AIDS. These numbers contradict the idea that "safe sex" has prevented HIV from spreading.

Does HIV Take Years to Cause AIDS?

For more than a decade, scientists throughout the world agreed that HIV had a latency period, a time during which it remained inactive before becoming active and causing immune destruction. The notion of a latency period was used to explain why HIV did not behave like all other infectious, disease-causing microbes that cause illness soon after infection, and why significant quantities of active HIV could not be found in people who test HIV positive.

At first, HIV's latency period was thought to be a few months long. It was then revised to one year, then two, then three and five years. As greater numbers of people who tested

HIV positive did not develop AIDS as predicted, the latency period was extended to ten or fifteen years, and more recently, even to entire lifetimes.

Just when HIV's growing latency period became the focus of mounting scrutiny, it was replaced with the concept of constantly active HIV that replicates and destroys cells at spectacular rates, a hypothesis known as "viral load." The media, government health agencies, AIDS organizations, and most AIDS doctors have uncritically accepted the viral load concept as fact. Proponents of viral load assert that HIV is rampant and destructive from the very moment of infection, and that the immune system of a person who tests positive is engaged in a perpetual struggle to keep the virus under control. They claim that HIV, after five, ten or fifteen years, eventually wins the battle by wearing out the immune system.

Viral load relies entirely on conclusions drawn from polymerase chain reaction (PCR) tests, and is based on the erroneous notion that the fragments of genetic material PCR finds correspond to counts of actual virus. In fact, PCR is unable to detect actual virus; it only amplifies genetic material associated with HIV (RNA or DNA), and the "load" produced by the test is a mathematical calculation, not a count of infectious virus. When standard methods of virus counting are applied, a viral load of 100,000 has been shown to correspond to less than ten infectious units of HIV, an amount that is far too small to induce illness.

Contrary to popular belief, PCR cannot determine what portion, if any, of the genetic material it detects represents infectious virus. In fact more than 99% of what PCR measures is noninfectious. Dr. Kary Mullis, who won the 1993 Nobel Prize for inventing PCR, is a member of The Group for the Scientific Reappraisal of the HIV/AIDS Hypothesis and refutes those who claim that HIV is the causative agent of AIDS.

"*Most researchers believe that the 'bush-meat trade' allowed the HIV-1 virus, and separately, HIV-2, to enter the human bloodstream.*"

HIV Spread to Humans Through the Cameroon Bushmeat Trade

Mary Carmichael

Early in the AIDS epidemic, researchers identified close similarities between the two species of the human immunodeficiency virus, HIV-1 and HIV-2, and simian immunodeficiency virus (SIV), a disease of chimpanzees and monkeys. In the following viewpoint, Mary Carmichael explains that SIV most likely jumped to humans, and began to mutate and evolve as HIV, about seventy-five years ago, when African hunters who captured Cameroon chimpanzees and sooty mangabeys for food or commercial purposes were infected through contact with animal blood. When isolated parts of Africa were connected by roads and urbanization and international travel boomed, Carmichael argues, the conditions were right for sudden, widespread human-to-human transmission of HIV. Mary Carmichael is a science writer based in Boston.

As you read, consider the following questions:

1. What evidence led researchers to conclude exactly where, and exactly which chimpanzee populations, HIV came from, according to Carmichael?

2. How did virologist Bette Korber calculate that HIV jumped from chimpanzee to humans shortly before 1931, according to the author?

3. What weaknesses does Carmichael identify in the competing theory that HIV jumped to humans from oral polio vaccine, cultivated in chimpanzee cells containing SIV and administered to millions of Africans in the late 1950s?

The theory [of the origins of HIV] rests on facts, and at least a few of them are undisputed—including, most significantly, HIV's family tree. There are two species of the virus, HIV-1 and HIV-2. The first evolved from a simian immunodeficiency virus (SIV) found in chimpanzees, while the second came from an SIV in a type of monkey called the sooty mangabey.

More than One Kind of HIV

HIV-1, which is responsible for the vast majority of AIDS cases worldwide, is divided into three groups—the "major" group M, and the much rarer "outlier" group O and "new" group N—that have diverged over years of mutation and evolution. Within the M group—which makes up 90 percent of all infections worldwide—there are at least nine strains, known as "clades," of HIV-1 that are constantly mutating and merging with each other, creating yet more new varieties. "The M group epidemiologically has overwhelmed what else is out there," says Dr. Beatrice Hahn of the University of Alabama-Birmingham, who has conducted much of the research into HIV's origin. HIV-2, on the other hand, is not as virulent and largely confined to West Africa, where it originated.

In May 2006, an international group of researchers led by Hahn answered two major questions about the origin of HIV-1 M, the deadliest and most widespread form of the virus: Where was its cradle, and what kind of chimp did it come from? Answering the questions was literally messy work—researchers collected 599 waste samples from wild chimpanzees and analyzed the viral particles they contained—but the results were immaculate. Three populations of *Pan troglodytes troglodytes* living in southern Cameroon provided the crucial data. Two of those populations currently carry SIVs that are molecular dead ringers for HIV-1 M, while many chimps in the third group are infected with an SIV remarkably similar to HIV-1 N. Group O's simian sibling is probably lurking in other chimp populations in West Central Africa, says Hahn, adding that she has "a pretty good idea where it's going to be . . . and we're going to find it."

The research puts to rest decades of speculation about the birthplace of most types of HIV and their animal "reservoir" in the wild. But there are still many questions that haven't yet been definitively settled.

When Did HIV-1 First Start Spreading in Humans?

HIV-1 is surprisingly old, and it probably "debuted" in humans at least three separate times—one for each subtype, M, N, and O. Scientists' best guess is that the precursor of the most common "M" virus jumped from the Cameroon chimps to humans sometime before 1931. Using samples of HIV-infected tissue harvested over the last three decades, virologist Dr. Bette Korber of Los Alamos National Laboratory has calculated that an ancestral form of HIV started spreading, slowly at first, in humans about 75 years ago. The actual jump from chimps to humans probably occurred shortly before that, says Hahn: "There's no reason to believe this was just lingering around in people."

Korber's model estimates a virus's age based on how extensively different strains have mutated. HIV is an unusual virus; it changes its DNA by both mutation and, more often, recombination, when two strains merge within the body and exchange genetic material. Some scientists refer to this process as "viral sex," and it may partially explain why it is so hard for scientists to make a treatment or vaccine. Korber's model does not take recombination into account, but given a virus's DNA configuration, it can roughly predict the age of that strain. Korber has tested the oldest known HIV sample, taken in 1959, and derived the 1931 estimate.

Why do scientists look at recent samples of HIV to determine the virus's overall age? Wouldn't it be better to use older samples that haven't had as much time to mutate? It would, but scientists don't have that luxury. Other than the 1959 sample, there are very few preserved specimens of HIV-infected tissue that predate the early '80s, when the virus was first recognized by health authorities. Researchers still hope there are forgotten samples in African freezers. "There has to be some serum or plasma somewhere, and given modern technology we could fish out the virus," says Dr. David Ho, director of the Aaron Diamond AIDS Research Center and one of the world's leading authorities on HIV.

But even if those samples are found someday, they won't necessarily yield definite answers about the virus's age, says Korber: "Often, you can't get anything out of samples like that." Most African samples are made of blood serum, and serum samples contain viral RNA, which degrades much faster than the DNA found in tissue samples. In fact, says Ho, the 1959 sample, which was sequenced by his laboratory, was kept in a freezer but still didn't survive the ravages of time. "It was completely dried up," he says. "We were only able to get small pieces [of genetic material], and we had to stitch them together."

Bushmeat Breeds New HIV

The HIV virus has jumped from primates to people on at least seven separate occasions in recent history, not twice as is commonly thought.

And people in Cameroon are showing up with symptoms of HIV, but are testing negative for both the virus and its primate equivalent SIV, the virus from which HIV is thought to have evolved. That suggests that new strains of an HIV-like virus are circulating in wild animals and infecting people who eat them, sparking fears that such strains could fuel an already disastrous global HIV pandemic.

Amitabh Avasthi, "Bushmeat Trade Breeds New HIV,"
New Scientist.com, August 9, 2004.

How Did HIV Infect Humans?

Most AIDS researchers believe that the "bushmeat trade" allowed the HIV-1 virus, and separately HIV-2, to enter the human bloodstream several times. Hunters who kill and butcher chimps and monkeys are regularly exposed to animal blood teeming with SIVs. If the hunters have cuts, bites, or scratches—and given the nature of their work they almost always do—they can catch the viruses from their prey. Hunters going after chimps in Cameroon could have caught the first strains of HIV-1. Sooty mangabeys, hunted and kept as pets in West Africa, could have transmitted HIV-2 to humans.

Africans have hunted chimps and monkeys and kept them as pets for centuries; they've presumably been exposed to SIVs during most of that time. But the conditions needed for HIV to spread widely weren't in place until after the continent was colonized and urbanized. The first victims would have found it easier to unwittingly spread the virus to sexual partners far and wide as roads and vehicles started connecting previously isolated villages and cities. Hospitals may have played a role, too. Strapped for cash, some of them probably re-used dirty needles, unknowingly infecting patients in the process.

Arguments Against the Competing Oral Polio Vaccine Theory

There are several competing theories, ranging from implausible conspiracies to arguments grounded in extensive research. The best-known of the latter, the "OPV/AIDS" theory, was exhaustively detailed in the 1999 book *The River*, by author Edward Hooper. As many as a million Africans were given oral polio vaccines (OPV) between 1957 and 1960. Hooper says witnesses have told him that a few batches of those vaccines were "grown" in chimps cells at a lab in Kisangani, a city in the Democratic Republic of the Congo—and that the chimp cells, and thus the vaccines, could have contained SIVs that jumped into humans. "There are highly significant correlations between the places where this vaccine was administered and the places where . . . AIDS first appeared on the planet four to 20 years later," Hooper says.

The majority of HIV researchers subscribe to the bushmeat theory and raise several arguments against the OPV theory, Hahn's recent research confirming that HIV-1 M and N arose from *Pan troglodytes troglodytes* chimps in Cameroon presents one problem: The Kisangani lab is in the Democratic Republic of the Congo, and it's home to a different subspecies of chimp than the one that was the source of HIV-1 M and N. However, it is possible that the chimps used in the Kisangani experiments were not from the area. In the spring of 2006, Hooper found a paper indicating that at least one of eight chimps at the Kisangani lab was a *Pan troglodytes troglodytes*.

The 1959 sample also presents a problem for the OPV theory. Judging by how fast the virus mutates, it had already diverged significantly from its SIV ancestors by the time doctors extracted it from a patient. However, the African polio vaccination program had begun only two years earlier, so under the OPV theory, the virus would have had only those two years in which to evolve. Dr. Ho, who sequenced the sample, says it looks like the virus has been around a lot longer than that.

"There is a highly significant correlation between the places where [oral polio vaccine] was fed, and the first appearances of HIV-1 . . . and of pandemic AIDS."

HIV Spread to Humans Through African Oral Polio Vaccines

Edward Hooper

In the following viewpoint, Edward Hooper argues that humankind accidentally sparked the AIDS epidemic through African trials of an experimental oral polio vaccine (OPV) in the late 1950s. Hooper claims that the OPV was cultivated in African laboratories using chimpanzee cells that contained simian immunodeficiency virus (SIV), the precursor to HIV, which was transferred to humans when the vaccine was given to a million Africans. According to Hooper, the first cases of AIDS subsequently appeared where the vaccine was administered. Edward Hooper is the author of Slim *(1990), an account of the East African AIDS epidemic, and* The River *(1999), a detailed presentation of the controversial OPV/AIDS theory.*

Edward Hooper, "The Bushmeat Theorists Fail to Deliver Once Again," *AIDSOrigins*, March 28, 2006. Reproduced by permission of Edward Hooper at www.aidsorigins.com.

As you read, consider the following questions:

1. Using the example of virologist Pierre Lepine's experimental trials, how does Hooper suggest the blood-borne virus HIV was transmitted to humans by an oral vaccine?

2. Why do scientists, established journals, and many people involved in the polio vaccine trials reject evidence that supports the OPV/AIDS theory, in Hooper's opinion?

3. What weaknesses does Hooper identify in the competing theory that HIV jumped from African chimpanzees to humans around 1930 through the butchering of bushmeat?

One of the earlier articles [published by Drs. Nathan Wolfe and Donald Burke, in 2004,] entitled "Naturally acquired simian retrovirus infections in central African hunters" reported significant levels (10 of 1,099 = 1%) of simian foamy virus (SFV) infection among Cameroonians from nine villages sited close to natural non-human primate habitats who reported direct contact with the blood or body fluids of wild non-human primates, "mainly through hunting and butchering." The article theorised that SIVs could also be transmitted to humans in this way, but it did not report the detection of any human infections with SIVs. . . .

Although their data suggests that Africans may perhaps be occasionally exposed to SIVs through cutting up bushmeat, they have as yet provided no evidence that such SIVs either replicate in humans, or cause productive infections.

Few would deny the theoretical possibilities that human exposures to SIVs through bushmeat might sometimes occur, or even that such exposures might sometimes cause productive infections. What is at issue is whether such human infections with SIV (if indeed they occur), are likely to have sparked either epidemic outbreaks, or the AIDS pandemic. . . .

The lack of evidence of any HIV infections prior to the 1950s suggests that the hand of modern man, or, more specifically, the hand of modern medical man (i.e., iatrogenic factors), may have played a key role. . . .

Polio Vaccines Were Cultivated in African Primates

During the 1950s, the approved standardisation procedures for polio vaccines allowed for them to be cultivated in the cells of any viable primate, and although most such vaccines were prepared in the cells of Asian monkeys such as the rhesus and cynomolgus macaques, vaccines prepared in the cells of several species of African primates were also used in a surprisingly large number of human trials. As we now know, several of these African primate species are host to their own SIVs.

Let me give just one example. From 1955 onwards the ancestral host to HIV-2, the sooty mangabey, *Cercocebus atys*, was one of many primates that were used for polio vaccine testing and propagation. The Pasteur Institute vaccine that was used in Europe was an inactivated polio vaccine (IPV), and was prepared mainly from the cells of *Papio papio*, the Guinea baboon, originating from West Africa. Large numbers of baboons were captured and held in collective pens at the Pasteur Institute facility at Pastoria, near Kindia in present-day Guinea Conakry. However, other "small monkeys" were also held in these same pens, and these included sooty mangabeys. A Guinean scientist who worked at Pastoria in the 1950s and who directed the facility from 1961 onwards has informed me that starting in 1956, Pasteur-produced polio vaccines were administered on a large scale by injection in French West Africa. (From 1955 to 1958, the Pasteur Institute's director of virology, Pierre Lepine, wrote several articles about the comparative benefits of killed and live polio vaccines, in the course of which he discussed the possibility of administering a third dose of attenuated vaccine, after establishing immunity with two prior injections of inactivated vaccine. He indicated that he and his colleagues had "conducted experiments along these lines, and we continue them, but we can only proceed with very great prudence and much deliberation.") One of the ways that Lepine proposed administering this live vaccine dose was, rather surprisingly, by injection, rather than by mouth. According to the Guinean scientist, this regime of injecting two doses of inactivated polio vaccine followed by one injection of live polio vaccine was indeed employed in French West Africa shortly after 1956.

Apart from man and the sooty mangabey, it seems that the only other African primate that can be persistently infected with HIV-2-like viruses is the baboon. There are therefore two potential ways in which vaccine stock used in Africa in the 1950s could have become infected with the HIV-2 precursor. A batch or batches could have been prepared direct from the cells of an SIV-infected sooty mangabey, or a batch or batches could have been prepared from baboons that had been co-caged with sooty mangabeys, and infected with SIV from the latter species via bites or scratches. . . .

Similarly the ancestral host of HIV-1, the common chimpanzee, *Pan troglodytes*, was among the primates that were collected in large numbers at both Franceville and at Gamaba farm (near Brazzaville), in French Equatorial Africa, in the second half of the 1950s. It is reported that cells from primates at Gamaba were used to "grow poliovirus" in the Pasteur Institute lab in Brazzaville from 1957 onwards, at a time when scientists based at that lab were conducting human trials of both IPV and OPV [oral polio vaccine] in French Equatorial Africa. At least one of the trials of an injected vaccine took place in 1957 at Mitzic (in the north of present-day Gabon) and in the eastern part of the contiguous territory of Spanish Guinea (now Equatorial Guinea), in an area which lies adjacent to the mooted hearths of the "minor variants of HIV-1", Groups O and N, in southern Cameroon. The earliest

Dismissing the OPV/AIDS Theory Is Dangerous

According to [eminent evolutionary biologist Bill Hamilton] the implications of [the OPV] hypothesis were dreadful. As he wrote in a letter to a colleague of the Royal Society, in October 1999: "The AIDS disaster, if the OPV theory is right (I rate the chance at about 95%), arose out of well-meaning (though also, it must be said, egotistical and profit-seeking) medical motives. But, the potential compounding of this, through failure to find the truth, to publicize and to study what happened, is that medical science continues virtually unwarned towards other equal—or conceivably greater—disasters."

The "greater disasters" that Bill had in mind were the effects of unknown viruses contaminating live animal products which are administered to our bodies in modern medical treatments. Bill's concern was that the basic evolutionary knowledge of the long-term consequences of these treatments is very poor in the medical industry.

Maria Luisa Bozzi, "Truth and Science," AIDSOrigins, 2003.
www.aidsorigins.com.

known infectee with HIV-1 Group O, a Norwegian sailor, appears to have become infected during a trip to Yaounde, Cameroon, in the winter of 1961–2.hellip;

AIDS First Appeared Where OPV Was Administered

There is a highly significant correlation between the places where the OPV (CHAT) [developed from Belgian Congo Chimps by Polish American Scientist Hilary Koprowski] was fed, and the first appearances of HIV-1 Group M, and of pandemic AIDS. The first evidence of HIV-1 Group M virus comes from a blood sample obtained from a male subject in Leopoldville (Kinshasa), allegedly in 1959, although the precise history of this blood sample is unclear, and it may in reality have been drawn between one to four years later. The age of the male subject is also unknown and, in contrast to previous reports, it is quite possible that he was a child at the time that his blood was tested. If so, then he would presumably have also been a CHAT vaccinee, for all Leopoldville children aged up to five years were vaccinated with CHAT between August 1958 and April 1960. The earliest death from Group M-related AIDS seems to have occurred in 1962.

Since the emergence of the OPV/AIDS theory, the great majority of the persons involved with these polio vaccine trials energetically deny that they ever prepared human polio vaccines from local primate tissues, but their accounts are characterised by internal contradictions and provable errors. Moreover, their versions of events are contradicted by an ever-increasing number of witnesses to, and participants in, these events. However, the CHAT vaccine-makers have been supported by many present-day virologists and public health officials, even if these individuals do not have first-hand experience of the vaccine trials. Many of these individuals, however, have research interests and public health preoccupations which coincide rather closely with the disproving of the controversial or "ugly" theory of OPV/AIDS. They apparently fear that if the AIDS pandemic should ever come to be directly linked to inappropriate medical experimentation, then popular faith in public health initiatives, such as vaccination campaigns, may be irrevocably shaken.

Disputing Critics of the OPV Theory

Several alleged "refutations" of the OPV theory of AIDS origin have been broadcast in science magazines and in the medical literature, but none of these refutations have been supported by any hard data. The most popular "refutations" are the following: (a) that batches of CHAT have been tested, and found to be free of HIV, SIV and chimpanzee DNA; (b) that phylogenetic dating analysis proves that the most recent common ancestor (MRCA) of HIV-1 existed in or around 1931, twenty or more years before the OPV trials. . . .

Yet on closer examination, none of these arguments hold water.

(a) The CHAT vaccine samples that were belatedly released for molecular analysis were all produced or prepared in the USA, whereas the vaccine batches that need to be released (if they still exist) and tested are those that were prepared in Africa, for instance in Stanleyville.

(b) Phylogenetic dating analysis is an inappropriate technique for measuring the evolution of a lentiretrovirus such as HIV: It measures only evolution by mutation, whereas 90% of the evolution of the HIVs occurs through recombination. Such attempts to date HIV by a molecular clock are innately bogus. . . .

Doctors Burke and Wolfe are not alone in their assumption that the AIDS pandemic virus, HIV-1 Group M, must have evolved through human contact with chimpanzee bushmeat, but their conclusions are, to say the least, premature. Any sincere approach to unravelling the origins of the HIVs must continue to examine the history of the experimental polio vaccines that were administered in the Belgian Congo, and elsewhere in sub-Saharan Africa, during the second half of the 1950s.

> "I believe HIV came out of animal can-
> cer research and dangerous vaccine and
> biological warfare experimentation."

HIV Is a Man-Made Product of Genetic Engineering and Medical Research

Alan Cantwell

Alan Cantwell, a retired American dermatologist, has been an active AIDS conspiracy theorist since the 1980s. In the following viewpoint, Cantwell speculates that HIV is actually the product of biowarfare experimentation carried out under cover of bona fide cancer and vaccine research. In particular, he accuses government agencies of introducing HIV into the gay communities of New York and other major cities via hepatitis-B vaccine programs from 1978–1980, and of activating a "dormant" AIDS virus in black Africans via World Health Organization–sponsored smallpox vaccine programs during the 1970s.

As you read, consider the following questions:

1. According to the author, where was HIV genetically engineered?

2. What evidence does Cantwell offer to support his claim that the strain of HIV found in American AIDS cases could not have originated in Africa?

3. In Cantwell's scenarios, why would government agencies test a new retrovirus on African blacks and American homosexuals?

The mixing of AIDS facts and fallacies has long been apparent to researchers like myself who are convinced that HIV did not come from Mother Nature and "species jumping," but was most likely introduced via contaminated vaccine experiments exclusively targeting the Black African and the American Gay community. . . .

Genetic Engineering and the AIDS Epidemic

There is a close connection between the rise of genetic engineering and mixing of viruses in the early 1970s and the outbreak of HIV in the late 1970s. This connection persists in the form of the many unprecedented "emerging diseases" caused by "new viruses" that continue up to the present time.

In 1970 the discovery of a cell enzyme, called "reverse transcriptase" by Howard Temin and David Baltimore, allowed molecular biologists to detect so-called retroviruses in some animal cancers. It was soon recognised that retroviruses could be found normally in the genes of many animal cells, and that scientists could manipulate these viruses to produce detrimental effects on the immune system. In "species jumping" laboratory experiments, many viruses were transferred between different animal species and were also adapted to human cells.

As part of President Richard Nixon's "War on Cancer," genetic engineering of viruses became an integral part of the now largely forgotten Special Virus Cancer Program, conducted under the auspices of the NCI [National Cancer Institute]. Nixon also transferred part of the Army's biological warfare unit at Fort Detrick, Maryland, over to the NCI, thereby allowing secret biowarfare experimentation to be carried out under cover of bona fide cancer research.

All this virus transfer and molecular manipulation was a biologic disaster waiting to happen. What would happen if one of these highly dangerous genetic creations escaped from the laboratory into the public sector? This culminated in a historic conference entitled "Biohazards in Biological Research" held at Asilomar, near Pacific Grove in California in 1973. Despite the biologic dangers, it was decided to continue this research.

By the late 1970s the War against Cancer and the Virus Cancer Program proved a bust, with no cancer-causing retroviruses found in humans. The Program was winding down in 1978, at the exact time when government scientists were also enrolling thousands of gay men in New York City to serve as guinea pigs in the hepatitis B experiment that took place that same year at the New York Blood Centre [NYBC] in Manhattan. In 1979 the first cases of AIDS in gay men were reported from Manhattan. Coincidence? I think not. . . .

The Gay Vaccine Experiment and the Outbreak of AIDS

The earliest AIDS cases in America can be clearly traced back to the time period when the hepatitis B experiment began at the New York Blood Centre. The Centre began injecting gay men with multiple doses of the experimental vaccine in November 1978. The inoculations ended in October 1979, less than two years before the official start of the epidemic. Most importantly, the vaccine was developed in chimpanzees—the primate now thought to contain the "ancestor" virus of HIV. Also downplayed is the Centre's pre-AIDS connection to primate research in Africa and also to a primate centre in the New York City area. The final experimental vaccine was also made by [pharmaceutical company] Merck and the [National Institutes of Health] NIH from the pooled serum specimens of countless gay men who carried the hepatitis B virus in their blood. . . .

Conspiracy Theories Abound for the Origins of AIDS

A number of conspiracy theorists have suggested that AIDS is actually a *man-made* disease. These theories often state that the disease was meant to deliberately wipe out a certain segment of the population in an act of genocide.

Dr. Boyd E. Graves postulates that AIDS was the culmination of biowarfare research conducted by the U.S. Government (and later, by the Soviet government) throughout the 20th century. He believes AIDS was developed and proliferated for the primary purpose of wiping out blacks, gays, and other social groups considered to be "excess population." Dr. Graves has also suggested that Gulf War syndrome may be related to AIDS, and that an effective cure for AIDS has already been developed and patented (United States Patent 5,676,977) by a company called Antelman Technologies Ltd., but is being withheld.

SourceWatch, *"AIDS Conspiracy," Center for Media and Democracy, January 24, 2006.*

The hepatitis B experiment, which inoculated over 1,000 healthy gay men, was a huge success, with 96% of the men developing antibodies against the hepatitis virus. This high rate of success could not have been achieved if the men were immunosuppressed, because immunosuppressed people do not easily form antibodies to the vaccine. The experiment was followed by similar hepatitis B experiments using gay men in Los Angeles, San Francisco, Chicago, Denver and St. Louis, beginning in March 1980 and ending in October 1981, the same year the epidemic became official.

In the mid-1980s the many blood specimens donated by the gay Manhattan men during the experiment were retrospectively examined for HIV infection by researchers at the

NYBC. It was determined that 6% of the specimens donated between 1978–1979 were positive for HIV. By 1984 (the end of the study period) over 40% of the men tested positive for HIV. . . .

There is also a suppressed connection between the outbreak of AIDS in Africa and the widespread vaccine programs conducted by the World Health Organization (WHO) in the 1970s in Central Africa, particularly the smallpox eradication program. On May 11, 1987, *London Times* science writer Pearce Wright suggested the smallpox vaccine program could have awakened a "dormant" AIDS virus infection in Africa. [Robert] Gallo [the American scientist who first announced the link between HIV and AIDS in 1984] was quoted as saying, "The link between the WHO program and the epidemic is an interesting and important hypothesis. I cannot say that it actually happened, but I have been saying for some years that the use of live vaccines, such as that used for smallpox, can activate a dormant infection such as HIV." . . .

Medical Experimentation and Biological Warfare

The idea of man-made AIDS is often considered a paranoid belief. Why would scientists introduce a virus to kill millions of people? AIDS experts routinely blame primates and human sexuality for the origin and spread of HIV, but they never consider the possibility that HIV could have originated in an animal cancer virus laboratory.

The sad truth is that governments and the military do indeed experiment on unsuspecting citizens. . . . It is clear that AIDS started as a "gay disease." However, yet another downplayed fact is that the HIV "strain" in America is different from the HIV strains found in Africa.

Harvard virologist Max Essex claims the American HIV strain spreads more easily via anal sex; whereas the African strains spread more efficiently via vaginal sex. This could explain why the American epidemic spreads primarily through homosexual activity and anal sex, while in Africa it is primarily heterosexual and spreads through vaginal sex. The "different" HIV strain in America is further evidence that "American AIDS" did *not* originate in Africa. . . .

I believe HIV came out of animal cancer research and dangerous vaccine and biological warfare experimentation—and that HIV made its way into vaccines injected into African Blacks and American Gays. If unrecognised cancer microbes are proven to be an unrecognised infectious factor in cancer and AIDS, as I believe they are, this would certainly add to the dangers of genetic engineering of cancer viruses and new bio-warfare agents. . . .

Is AIDS Genocide Against Gays and Blacks?

Why is there a blackout of the man-made theory of AIDS in the scientific literature and in the corporate-controlled media? . . .

I do not believe the exclusive introduction of HIV into the most hated minority in America was caused by monkeys in the African bush, particularly when AIDS appeared immediately after the gay experiment. Why are primates in the African wild blamed when tens of thousands of captive primates in virus labs all over the world have been injected with infectious viruses and cancerous tissue for more than a century?

Why were African Blacks targeted? Many Africans and African-Americans believe AIDS is an experiment to rid the world of Black people, as part of a government-sanctioned world depopulation program.

American gays were the perfect target to test a new retrovirus. A largely homophobic public would easily accept HIV infection in gays, due to their purported promiscuity and drug use. Few people would believe the US government would secretly test biologic agents on its civilians, although there is a well-documented history of secret unethical experimentation extending back to the Cold War of the 1950s which includes the government's horrendous "radiation experiments."

I cannot explain the silence and apathy on these issues from the Black and the Gay communities. People don't seem to care much about genocide unless their own group is affected; and even so, most people are in denial and don't want to know about man-made AIDS. Many AIDS activists simply dismiss the man-made theory as a "distraction" which interferes with HIV testing and treatment, and the search for a cure.

> "Heterosexual intercourse is now respon-
> sible for 70–80% of all HIV transmis-
> sions worldwide."

HIV Is Primarily Transmitted Through Heterosexual Intercourse

Nancy Padian

Nancy Padian is a professor of obstetrics, gynecology, and repro-
ductive sciences at the University of California, San Francisco;
director of international programs at the UCSF AIDS Research
Institute; and an expert in the heterosexual transmission of HIV
and other sexually transmitted diseases. In 1997 she coauthored
a paper published in the American Journal of Epidemiology
that AIDS denialists tout as evidence that HIV is not *hetero-*
sexually transmitted. In the following viewpoint, Padian sets the
record straight: Studies show that HIV certainly and primarily is
transmitted heterosexually; claims to the contrary are a myth;
references to "the Padian paper" in support of that myth are a
misuse of her data; and the notion that her work has been sup-
pressed by other AIDS researchers is absurd.

Nancy Padian, "Heterosexual Transmission of HIV," *American Journal of Epidemiol-*
ogy, vol. 146, 1997. Copyright © 1997 by The Johns Hopkins University School of Hygiene and Public Health. Republished with permission of The Johns Hopkins University
School of Hygiene and Public Health, conveyed through Copyright Clearance Center,
Inc.

As you read, consider the following questions:

1. What is the likelihood of male-to-female HIV infection after a single exposure, according to Padian?

2. What factors raise the likelihood of heterosexual transmission of HIV to 20 percent or higher, according to the author?

3. In what way is misunderstanding the risk of heterosexual HIV transmission like playing Russian roulette, in Padian's view?

HIV is unquestionably transmitted through heterosexual intercourse. Indeed, heterosexual intercourse is now responsible for 70–80% of all HIV transmissions worldwide. The current likelihood of male-to-female infection after a single exposure to HIV is 0.01–0.32%, and the current likelihood of female-to-male infection after a single exposure is 0.01–0.1%. These estimates are mostly derived from studies in the developed world. However, a man or a woman can become HIV-positive after just one sexual contact. In developing countries, particularly those in sub-Saharan Africa, several factors (co-infection with other sexually transmitted diseases, circumcision practices, poor acceptance of condoms, patterns of sexual partner selection, locally circulating viral subtypes, high viral loads among those who are infected, etc.) can increase the likelihood of heterosexual transmission to 20% or even higher. Evidence that specifically documents the heterosexual transmission of HIV comes from studies of HIV-discordant couples (i.e., couples in a stable, monogamous relationship where one partner is infected and the other is not); over time, HIV transmission occurs. Other studies have traced the transmission of HIV through networks of sexual partners. Additional evidence comes from intervention studies that, for example, promote condom use or encourage reductions in the numbers of sexual partners: The documented success of these interventions is because they prevent the sexual transmission of HIV.

Male Circumcision Can Reduce Heterosexual HIV Spread

U.N. health agencies recommended [in March 2007] that heterosexual men undergo circumcision because of "compelling" evidence that it can reduce their chances of contracting HIV by up to 60 percent. . . .

"The recommendations represent a significant step forward in HIV prevention," said Dr. Kevin De Cock, director of WHO's HIV/AIDS department. "Countries with high rates of heterosexual HIV infection and low rates of male circumcision now have an additional intervention which can reduce the risk of HIV infection in heterosexual men."

Associated Press, "Circumcision Urged to Fight HIV,"
MSNBC.com, *March 28, 2007.*

In short, the evidence for the sexual transmission of HIV is well documented, conclusive, and based on the standard, uncontroversial methods and practices of medical science. Individuals who cite the 1997 Padian et al. publication or data from other studies by our research group in an attempt to substantiate the myth that HIV is not transmitted sexually are ill informed, at best. Their misuse of these results is misleading, irresponsible, and potentially injurious to the public.

Practicing Safe Sex Only Lowers a Very Real Risk

A common practice is to quote out of context a sentence from the Abstract of the 1997 paper: "Infectivity for HIV through heterosexual transmission is low." Anyone who takes the trouble to read and understand the paper should appreciate that it reports on a study of behavioral interventions such as those mentioned above: Specifically, discordant couples were strongly counseled to use condoms and practice safe sex. That we witnessed no HIV transmissions after the intervention documents the success of the interventions in preventing the sexual transmission of HIV. The sentence in the Abstract reflects this success—nothing more, nothing less. Any attempt to refer to this or other of our publications and studies to bolster the fallacy that HIV is not transmitted heterosexually or homosexually is a gross misrepresentation of the facts and a travesty of the research that I have been involved in for more than a decade.

If safe sex practices are followed, and if there are no complicating factors such as those mentioned above, the risk of HIV transmission can be as low as our studies suggest ... IF. But many people misunderstand probability: They think that if the chance of misfortune is one in six, that they can take five chances without the likelihood of injury. This "Russian Roulette" misapprehension is dangerous to themselves and to others. Furthermore, complicating factors are often not evident or obvious in a relationship, so their perceived absence should not be counted on as an excuse not to practice safe sex.

Finally, it is a complete fallacy to allege or insinuate that this work has been "suppressed" or "ignored" by the AIDS community or unsupported by UCSF or any other institution with which I have worked. To the contrary, these findings have been seen as central and seminal to the problem of heterosexual transmission rates and the development of interventions to lower the rate of transmission and infection worldwide, many of which are being conducted by my research group. The success of my working group has been fueled, not hindered, by our research on the heterosexual transmission of HIV, attested to by our long record of peer-reviewed publications.

"It's so hard to spread HIV vaginally [because] the virus is unable to penetrate or infect healthy vaginal or cervical tissue."

Heterosexual Transmission of HIV Is Negligible

Michael Fumento

In the following viewpoint, Michael Fumento contradicts World Health Organization (WHO) estimates that most of the spread of HIV worldwide—and more than 90 percent of cases in Africa—occurs through heterosexual intercourse. On the contrary, Fumento maintains, HIV cannot infect healthy vaginal or cervical tissue. He accuses the scientific and medical establishment of failing to control the real vectors of the African epidemic: anal sex between men and contaminated needle punctures. Michael Fumento, a journalist specializing in health and science issues, is the author of The Myth of Heterosexual AIDS.

As you read, consider the following questions:

1. How does Fumento interpret epidemiologist Nancy Padian's study to support his claim that the risk of heterosexual HIV transmission is extremely low?

Michael Fumento, "Why Is HIV So Prevalent in Africa?" *Tech Central Station*, April 15, 2005. Copyright 2005 *Tech Central Station*. Reproduced by permission.

2. What evidence does the author present that homosexual practices are far more widespread in Africa than is acknowledged?

3. Fumento says the medical establishment fears being blamed for the deaths of millions if the actual source of most African HIV transmission is recognized; what are some of the common medical practices Fumento links to contaminated needle punctures?

Ninety-nine percent of AIDS and HIV cases in Africa come from sexual transmission, and virtually all is heterosexual. So says the World Health Organization, with other agencies toeing the line. Some massive condom airdrops accompanied by a persuasive propaganda campaign would practically make the epidemic vanish overnight. Or would it?

A determined renegade group of three scientists has fought for years—with little success—to get out the message that no more than a third of HIV transmission in Africa is from sexual intercourse and most of that is anal. By ignoring the real vectors, they say, we're sacrificing literally millions of people.

These men are no crackpots. John Potterat is author of 140 scholarly publications. He began working for the El Paso County, Colorado, health department in 1972 and initiated the first U.S. partner-tracing program for AIDS/HIV.

Stuart Brody, who has accepted [in 2005] a full professorship in Psychology at University of Paisley in Scotland, has published over 100 scholarly publications, including a book called *Sex at Risk*. Economist and anthropologist David Gisselquist has almost 60 scholarly publications to his name and is currently advising the government of India on staunching its potentially explosive epidemic.

Vaginal HIV Transmission Is Very Difficult

These renegades point out that a reason we know vaginal sex can't be the risk in Africa it's portrayed to be is that it hasn't been much of a risk in the U.S. Here 12 percent of AIDS cases are "attributed to" heterosexual transmission, meaning they *claimed* to have gotten it that way. Of these, over a third are males.

Yet San Francisco epidemiologist Nancy Padian evaluated 72 male partners of HIV-infected women over several years, during which time only one man was infected. Even in that case, there were "several instances of vaginal and penile bleeding during intercourse." So even the small U.S. heterosexual figure appears grossly exaggerated.

The chief reason it's so hard to spread HIV vaginally is that, as biopsies of vaginal and cervical tissue show, the virus is unable to penetrate or infect healthy vaginal or cervical tissue. Various sexually transmitted diseases allow vaginal HIV infection, but even those appear to increase the risk only by about 2–4 times.

So if vaginal intercourse can't explain the awful African epidemic, what can? Surely it's not homosexuality, since we've been told there is none in Africa. In fact, the practice has long been widespread.

For example, German anthropologist Kurt Falk reported in the 1920s that bisexuality was almost universal among the male populations of African tribes he studied. Medical records also show that African men who insist they're straighter than the proverbial arrow often suffer transmissible anorectal diseases.

Needle Punctures Are the Primary Vector in Africa

Yet almost certainly greater—and more controllable—contributors to the African epidemic are "contaminated punctures from such sources as medical injections, dental injections, surgical procedures, drawing as well as injecting blood, and rehydration through IV tubes," says Brody.

You don't even need to go to a clinic to be injected with HIV: Almost two-thirds of 360 homes visited in sub-Saharan

Substantial HIV Prevalence in Children Casts Doubt on Heterosexual Transmission

The assertion that heterosexual transmission accounts for over 90% of HIV in African adults lacks supporting empirical evidence linking HIV to sexual behaviors. The evidence WHO/UNAIDS uses to buttress the heterosexual paradigm is mostly indirect and circumstantial, and much of it seems aimed at debunking the role of health care rather than substantiating the role of heterosexual contact. For example, the [agency] asserts, "Children between 5 and 14 years, who are generally not sexually active yet, have very low infection rates." In fact, few surveys have screened for HIV in African children, and some (but not all) have reported substantial HIV prevalence. For example, 4.2% among urban children 6–15 years old in Rwanda in 1986 and 5.6% among 2–14-year-old children in a national survey in South Africa in 2002. These rates, which are much higher than could be expected from vertical transmission, point to other means of transmission, possibly health care transmission. It should be noted that observed rates are not likely due to substandard tests (Rwandan cases were confirmed by Western blot, and tests used in South Africa have over 99% specificity) or to child sexual abuse or early sexual activity.

David Gisselquist et al., "Examining the Hypothesis That Sexual Transmission Drives Africa's AIDS Epidemic,"
AIDScience, vol. 3., no. 10, 2003.

Africa had medical injection equipment that was apparently shared by family members. This, says Brody, can explain why both a husband and wife will be infected.

For those who care to look, there are many indicators that punctures play a huge role in the spread of disease. For example, during the 1990s HIV increased in Zimbabwe at approximately 12 percent annually, even as condom use increased and sexually transmitted infections rapidly fell.

Or consider that in a review of nine African studies, HIV prevalence in inpatient children ranged from 8.2% to 63%—as many as three times the prevalence in women who'd given birth. If the kids didn't get the virus from their mothers or from sex, whence its origin? Investigations of large clinical outbreaks in Russia, Romania, and Libya demonstrate HIV can be readily transmitted through pediatric health care.

Good people can differ on exactly how much of the HIV in Africa is spread vaginally—including our three renegades themselves. Nevertheless, their findings readily belie the official figures. AIDS studies in Africa, Potterat says, are "First World researchers doing second rate science in Third World countries."

Unwillingness to Abandon a False Belief

There's no one reason for the mass deception. In part, once people have established any paradigm it becomes much easier to justify than challenge.

"These guys are wearing intellectual blinders," says Potterat. "Only a handful are even looking at routes other than sex. They have sex on the brain." Other reasons:

- Grant money goes to those who follow the dictates of the paradigm, not to those challenging it. "Sex is sexy," notes Potterat.

- There's fear that blame for the epidemic will fall on the medical profession.

- To the extent vaginal sex does play a role in spreading the disease, there's fear people will stop worrying about it.

Finally, says Brody, for researchers to concede they were wrong would be "to admit they're complicit in mass death. That's hard to admit to yourself, much less to other people."

Hard, yes. And too late for many. But not too late for millions more in Africa and other underdeveloped nations—if we act now.

Periodical Bibliography

The following articles have been selected to supplement the diverse views presented in this chapter.

Michelle Andrews "HIV Screening for One and All," *U.S. News & World Report*, October 2, 2006.

Annals of Internal Medicine "Causes of Death in People with AIDS in New York City between 1999 and 2004," September 19, 2006.

Adele Baleta "Questioning of HIV Theory of AIDS Causes Dismay in South Africa," *Lancet*, April 1, 2000.

John Cohen "Merck Reemerges with a Bold AIDS Vaccine Effort," *Science*, April 6, 2001.

David Ehrenstein "A Planet Under Siege," *Advocate*, 2003.

Robert C. Gallo "We Can Whip AIDS," *Newsweek International*, November 28, 2005.

Leslie Hanna "Special Report on HIV & AIDS," *Bulletin of Experimental Treatments for AIDS*, Spring 2000.

John S. James "AIDS Denialists: How to Respond," *AIDS Treatment News*, May 5, 2000. www.thebody.com/content/art32141.html.

Donald G. McNeil Jr. "Epidemic Errors," *New York Times*, February 4, 2001.

National Institute of Allergy and Infectious Diseases "How HIV Causes AIDS," November 2004.

K. Porter and B. Zaba "The Empirical Evidence for the Impact of HIV on Adult Mortality in the Developing World: Data from Serological Studies," *AIDS*, June 18, 2004.

Mercedes Sayagues "Witchcraft, Vengeful Spirits and the Plague—The AIDS Battle Needs a New Approach," *Newsweek*, December 15, 2003.

OPPOSING
VIEWPOINTS®
SERIES

CHAPTER 3

How Can the Spread of AIDS Be Controlled?

Chapter Preface

The Controversy over the Safer Sex Movement

Those who work to stop the spread of AIDS have focused on a number of methods in hopes of achieving that goal. Some advocate developing an AIDS vaccine. Others believe wide-scale testing for HIV will stem further infection. Another method is to change the behaviors of at-risk groups such as sexually active teenagers or IV drug users. Yet another controversial method employed to stem the spread of HIV and other sexually transmitted diseases is "safer sex" education. "Safer sex" is a set of practices designed to reduce the risk of spreading infection during sexual contact.

The "safer sex" movement began in the 1980s shortly after AIDS was discovered. Once it became clear that HIV can be transmitted by sharing bodily fluids during sexual contact, AIDS activists and medical researchers wanted to find a way to stop AIDS without excluding all sexual activity. Education programs were initiated to promote the use of condoms and other prophylactics to protect sexual partners from exchanging bodily fluids. Some safer sex programs also promoted less risky behaviors such as masturbation and non-penetrative sex (sometimes called "outercourse"). Soon, public health educators adopted the safer-sex model, expanding it to include information about other sexually transmitted diseases (STDs) such as syphilis, gonorrhea, and genital herpes.

Not everyone approves of the safer-sex approach to preventing AIDS and other STDs. Some organizations, such as the Heritage Foundation and the Roman Catholic Church, oppose sexual intercourse outside of the context of marriage and procreation. They argue that safer sex programs that openly teach about condom use and other non-procreative sexual relations encourage what they see as immoral behavior. Abstinence programs and virginity pledges are favored by those opposed to the safer sex movement. Completely abstaining from sex before marriage, they assert, is the best protection against STDs *and* moral decline.

Proponents of safer sex education counter that promoting abstinence without also providing clear and accurate information about risky sex is irresponsible. Studies have shown, for example, that the majority of teenagers who pledge abstinence do end up having sex before marriage. They are also one-third less likely to use contraceptives than teens who have received safer sex education. Often the debate over abstinence vs. safer sex education turns on differing viewpoints about sexual knowledge. Abstinence-based programs assume that providing information about sex will encourage sexual behavior. Safer sex programs assume that many people will engage in sexual relations whether they are educated about it or not. If that is true, they argue, then teaching people about safer sex might just save their lives.

> *"A vaccine that is 50% effective, given to just 30% of the population, could reduce the number of new HIV infections . . . by more than half."*

An AIDS Vaccine Would Significantly Slow the Spread of AIDS

International AIDS Vaccine Initiative

In the following viewpoint, the International AIDS Vaccine Initiative (IAVI) argues that a vaccine is one of the best hopes for controlling the spread of HIV. Even if a vaccine was only partially effective, the IAVI maintains, it could reduce a person's susceptibility to HIV infection, reduce the likelihood that a vaccinated person who is later infected would transmit the virus to others, and slow the progression of AIDS in vaccinated individuals. The IAVI, a global nonprofit organization founded in 1996 and operating in twenty-three countries, works with a network of government and private-sector partners to research, develop, and test candidate HIV vaccines and to make an eventual vaccine accessible to all who need it.

International AIDS Vaccine Initiative, "Estimating the Impact of an AIDS Vaccine in Developing Countries," *IAVI Policy Brief #10*, November 2006. Reproduced by permission.

As you read, consider the following questions:

1. Why is an HIV vaccine needed even if ongoing AIDS prevention and treatment efforts are expanded, according to the IAVI?

2. In the three scenarios modeled by the IAVI, how many new infections would be averted even if a vaccine were only 30 percent effective? How many would be averted if the vaccine were 70 percent effective?

3. What alternative to vaccinating the entire adult population does the IAVI suggest would be nearly as effective?

Vaccines are consistently among the best tools for fighting infectious diseases. An AIDS vaccine should be considered one of the best hopes to end the spread of HIV. However, questions surrounding potential AIDS vaccines remain: how effective would an AIDS vaccine be? Would a vaccine still be needed if existing prevention programs and antiretroviral treatments are significantly expanded while a vaccine is still being developed? What will be the impact of first generation vaccines if they only provide partial protection against HIV?

To address these questions, The International AIDS Vaccine Initiative (IAVI) has been modeling the future epidemiology of the AIDS epidemic and the impact that a vaccine could have. This analysis shows that including vaccines as part of a comprehensive response can make a significant impact in ending the AIDS pandemic in the coming decades. Additionally, in order to yield significant benefits, a vaccine would not have to be 100% effective or reach 10% of an at risk population. A vaccine that is 50% effective, given to just 30% of the population, could reduce the number of new HIV infections in the developing world by more than half over 15 years. A vaccine that is more effective or reaches a greater number of people would have an even larger impact. . . .

The analysis described here used the following seven countries (in four regions) to build an estimate of the epidemiological impact of vaccines for the developing world as a whole: Nigeria and South Africa (Sub-Saharan Africa), Brazil and Mexico (Latin America), China and India (Asia), and Russia (Eastern Europe). These countries were selected because they are representative of the epidemic in their regions and because they are among the countries with the greatest absolute numbers of infections. Collectively, they contain 46% of people living with HIV and 70% of all new adult HIV infections in the developing world. . . .

First-Generation Vaccines May Only Provide Partial Protection

Although the exact level of protection that will be conferred by first-generation vaccines is still unknown, scientists believe they may only be partially effective in protecting against HIV. Based on the leading vaccine candidates currently being tested in clinical trials, an AIDS vaccine could have a combination of the following three mechanisms of action:

1. Protect the vaccinated individual against HIV infection (i.e., reduced susceptibility);
2. Reduce the probability that a vaccinated individual who later becomes infected will transmit his/her infection to others, (i.e., reduced infectiousness);
3. Slow the rate of progression from HIV infection to death in vaccinated individuals (i.e., increase in average survival time following infection).

All three of these possible effects are included in the three main scenarios (Low, Medium, and High) that were tested in the HIV vaccine model. Plausible ranges were chosen to reflect current understanding of AIDS vaccine science. Coverage levels were based on previous work that indicates uptake of a partially effective vaccine in the general population would be modest.

MRKAd5:
A Promising HIV Vaccine Candidate

[A] test vaccine, known as the MRKAd5 HIV-1 trivalent vaccine, . . . already has been studied for several years in phase I and II trials involving thousands of volunteers in the Americas, Africa, and Australia to evaluate safety and immune responses. In those previous trials this vaccine was found to be safe and to stimulate cellular immune responses against HIV in more than half of volunteers.

Merck Research Laboratories developed the test vaccine that is based on an adenovirus—a common cold virus that has been modified so that it cannot cause a cold in humans or be passed from person to person. The adenovirus is the carrier or vector which transports copies of three HIV genes called gag, pol, and nef. The vaccine is made in the laboratory and does not contain live HIV. The test vaccine therefore cannot cause infection.

The hope is that these HIV genes will produce a cellular immune response to HIV and cause the body to make killer cells that are programmed to recognize and destroy cells that are infected with HIV. The studies already completed with this vaccine suggest that it is generally well tolerated and that the response of the immune system or immunogenicity is high.

News-Medical.Net, *"South Africa Starts Major HIV/AIDS Vaccine Trial,"* February 11, 2007.

Partial Efficacy Vaccines Could Significantly Blunt the AIDS Epidemic

The results generated by this new model show that an AIDS vaccine could substantially alter the course of the AIDS pandemic and reduce the number of new infections, even if vaccine efficacy and population coverage levels are relatively low and other programs for treatment and prevention have been scaled up. The model also shows that an AIDS vaccine could significantly reduce the number of deaths attributable to AIDS. The reduction in AIDS mortality is smaller than the predicted decrease in new infections, because some deaths will be averted by expanded access to antiretroviral treatment.

With expanded prevention and treatment efforts but no vaccine (the Baseline scenario), the annual number of new adult HIV infections would decrease from approximately 4 million today to 3.2 million by 2015 and would grow slightly after that due to population growth. Seen in this context, a vaccine which is introduced a decade from now would make a big difference:

- In the *Low Impact* scenario, an AIDS vaccine with 30% efficacy provided to 20% of the population would avert 5.5 million new infections between 2015 and 2030 (11% of the infections that would otherwise be expected), lowering the annual number of new infections in 2030 by 17%.

- In the *Medium Impact* scenario, an AIDS vaccine with 50% efficacy provided to 30% of the population would avert 17 million new infections between 2015 and 2030 (35% of new infections that would otherwise occur), reducing the annual number of new infections in 2030 by more than half.

- In the *High Impact* scenario, an AIDS vaccine with 70% efficacy provided to 40% of the population would avert 28 million new infections between 2015 and 2030 (56% of new infections that would otherwise be expected), reducing the annual number of new infections in 2030 by 81%.

Economic Benefits of Vaccines

In addition to the humanitarian imperative, this analysis helps to illustrate the potential economic benefits of AIDS vaccines. In an environment of universal access to treatment, each infection averted by a vaccine translates into thousands of dollars saved in averted ART [antiretroviral therapy] costs.

In addition to the three scenarios listed above, several other possible scenarios were also examined:

- *More optimistic.* Higher levels of coverage yield dramatic results. For example, a vaccine with 70% efficacy provided to 70–90% of the population would reduce the number of new infections per year by 88–94%, nearly stopping the spread of AIDS.

- *Selective targeting.* The model suggests that targeting the vaccine to high-risk populations in countries with relatively modest epidemics still achieves 85% of the effect in terms of avoiding infections and saving lives, as compared to vaccinating the general adult population.

- *Incomplete achievement of universal access.* If [universal access to vaccinations is] not fully achieved, the magnitude of the AIDS epidemic would be greater than predicted in the baseline scenario, and the absolute impact of a vaccine would also be larger.

More Work Needs to Be Done

This modeling work shows that even a partially effective vaccine provided to a modest proportion of the population could lead to a major decrease in new HIV infections. Even if a vaccine is first introduced a decade from now in a world where other prevention and treatment activities have expanded, an AIDS vaccine will still make a significant impact. A highly effective vaccine coupled with broad coverage as a part of a comprehensive package of treatment and prevention could come close to stopping AIDS. This underscores the importance of sustaining investments and policy efforts to accelerate AIDS vaccine research and development.

"A vaccine against AIDS is becoming
little more than a pipe dream."

Prospects for an AIDS Vaccine Are Dim

Richard Horton

In the following viewpoint, British physician Richard Horton challenges claims that given enough time and money, researchers can develop a vaccine that can control the spread of HIV/AIDS. According to Horton, this flawed approach assumes a vaccine can overcome the enormous genetic variation, and mutability, of HIV—but no vaccine can stimulate antibodies to dozens of constantly evolving virus subtypes. Moreover, he argues, HIV defeats the ways a vaccine works: It can both "hide from" and ultimately destroy the antibodies a vaccine would produce. Richard Horton is editor of the Lancet, *a weekly medical journal based in London and New York, and a visiting professor at the London School of Hygiene and Tropical Medicine.*

As you read, consider the following questions:

1. How is HIV complex geographically as well as genetically, according to the author?

Richard Horton, "AIDS: The Elusive Vaccine," *New York Review of Books*, vol. 51, September 23, 2004. Copyright © 2004 by NYREV, Inc. Reprinted with permission from *The New York Review of Books*.

2. How many known subtypes and variants of HIV are there, by Horton's explanation?

3. How is HIV able to evade the antibodies a vaccine would produce, according to Horton?

After twenty-three years of intense research into the human immunodeficiency virus (HIV), together with the accumulated experience of more than twenty million deaths from the infection worldwide, there is still no prospect of a vaccine to prevent AIDS. Is the discovery of a vaccine simply a matter of time? Or has this virus presented scientists with a hitherto underestimated, perhaps even impossible, challenge?

The International AIDS Vaccine Initiative (IAVI), the world's largest single organization devoted to finding an AIDS vaccine, has argued that the obstacles to progress are clear and resolvable—lack of political commitment and inadequate scientific resources. With offices in New York, Amsterdam, Nairobi, and New Delhi, it has invested $100 million in the search for a vaccine. At the Bangkok AIDS conference held in July 2004, Seth Berkley, IAVI's president, argued that "only a vaccine can end the epidemic," that "a vaccine is achievable," and that spending on vaccine research must double to $1.3 billion annually in order to find it. "The world is inching toward a vaccine, when we should be making strides," he said. The present situation was little short of "a global disgrace."

But contrary to the predictions and promises of most AIDS experts, the signs are that a vaccine to prevent HIV infection will not be found for, at the very least, several decades to come—if at all. Those responsible for carrying on the global fight against AIDS do not accept this grim outlook, at least publicly. Yet it is a conclusion, based on all the evidence gathered so far, which increasingly defies rebuttal. Until the gravity of this scientific failure is openly acknowledged, a serious debate about how to end HIV's lethal grip on some of the poorest and most vulnerable human populations in the world cannot take place.

No Vaccine Protects Against
Dozens of Forms of HIV

The holy grail of AIDS prevention is a single-dose, safe, affordable, oral vaccine that gives lifelong protection against all subtypes of HIV. The first hurdle facing vaccine designers, therefore, is dealing with the extraordinary genetic complexity of the HIV epidemic.

HIV exists as two strains—HIV-1, which dominates the epidemic, and HIV-2, which is largely confined to West Africa. So far, at least ten different patterns of HIV-1 infection have been identified. These patterns reflect particular geographic and genetic profiles of viral spread. For example, HIV-1 subtype B (there are nine genetic subtypes) is the common form of the virus in North America and Western Europe. India, by contrast, is under threat from HIV-1 subtype C. In Africa, where some two thirds of those with HIV now live (about 25 million people) and where there were three million new infections in 2003 alone, the situation is more diverse.

Southern and eastern regions of the continent face a predominantly HIV-1 subtype C epidemic. Central Africa sees a highly mixed picture—HIV-1 subtypes A, D, F, G, H, J, and K. The implications of these differences for vaccine development remain uncertain. The best guess is that the genetic complexity of HIV will influence the effectiveness of any tested vaccine.

There are also over a dozen virus variants, called circulating recombinant forms, whose genomes have a structure that lies in between those of known subtypes. They also contribute to the difficulty of creating a one-size-fits-all vaccine. At present, scientists do not know if each subtype and every variant will need its own specific vaccine. It may well be that they will.

Worse still, a given subtype of the virus does not stay the same. HIV is continually evolving. The ingenuity of the virus in adapting to prevailing pressures in its environment—such

HIV: Tougher than Smallpox, Measles, and Polio

Perhaps the most discouraging problem facing vaccine researchers is that in the 25-plus years of the AIDS pandemic, not one individual has rid himself of the virus. As Dr. Anthony Fauci, head of the National Institute of Allergy and Infectious Diseases (NIAID), explains: "Of all the microbes we know of, this is the only one in which the body has proven itself completely incapable of eliminating the virus from the body once it gets infected. Even with the deadliest of diseases—the viruses of smallpox, of polio, of measles— you get infected, there's a certain mortality; then you clear the infection, the body gets an immune response, and it's unlikely you're going to get infected again. When you develop a vaccine, you look at the body and you say, 'This is what the body did to protect itself, and we're going to develop a vaccine that mimics what the body has done.' With HIV, the body has not been successful, so you don't have a framework to look and say, 'Ah, this is what we want to do.'"

"Finding a Cure: Is an AIDS Vaccine Out of Reach?"
Frontline: The Age of AIDS, *PBS, May 30, 2006.*

as the existence of a vaccine that triggers an attempt by the human body to eradicate it—is owing to an enzyme called reverse transcriptase. This enzyme is essential for viral replication, but it makes mistakes as it goes about its work. These mistakes, together with an extremely high rate of virus production, help HIV to produce an enormous family of genetically varied offspring.

Even if a vaccine were available, these different forms of HIV would almost certainly allow some of the virus to "escape" from any protective immune response that the human body mounted against it after vaccination. Some of these randomly generated "escape mutants," as they are called, would then be selected for survival in succeeding generations of the virus, since they would possess the advantage of being "fitter"—avoiding the body's immune response—than their non-mutated counterparts.

HIV Can Evade the Antibody Response Produced by Vaccines

These problems become easier to understand when one considers how a vaccine to prevent HIV infection would have to work if it was to produce what experts call sterilizing immunity—that is, complete protection from infection. The normal immune system has two ways of responding to infection. The first depends on the antibodies we all produce in our bodies. These large molecules bind to the virus particle and neutralize it, preventing HIV from going on to infect human cells. There are two critically important proteins on the surface of HIV-1, which are called gp120 and gp41. They are the means by which the virus enters human cells and they are the main targets of the neutralizing antibodies. The difficulty is that crucial parts of these surface molecules are hidden from the attacking antibodies. Such resilient viral topography, together with several molecular tricks that enable HIV to evade human defenses, severely weakens the body's immune response. Antibodies alone are therefore very unlikely to protect us from HIV.

The second response of the immune system involves not the production of antibodies but the rallying of cells to combat infection. There are two types of blood cell that are involved in an effective immune response to HIV—CD4+ and CD8+ T-lymphocytes, cells that develop within the thymus gland. The CD4+ cell is HIV's primary target. It is this cell type that is hit hardest by the virus, causing the typical immunodeficiency that characterizes AIDS. CD8+ cells—also called cytotoxic T-lymphocytes (CTLs)—matter because, among other actions, they kill cells that become infected with HIV. They are usually assisted in their task by CD4+ lymphocytes, which are, appropriately, also known as T-helper cells. This mopping-up operation has the potential to damp down the damage that HIV can do to the body.

Once a person is infected, a contest begins between the virus, which is trying to establish a foothold in the body, and the cellular immune response, which is trying to stop the virus from doing so. A vaccine should tip the balance of this contest in favor of the immune system by increasing the numbers of CD4+ and CD8+ cells that are poised to swing into action if HIV gains entry to the body at some point in the future.

HIV May Be Slowed But Not Stopped

In truth, a vaccine that strengthens this kind of cell-mediated immunity would probably not prevent infection. It would likely slow the rate at which the virus took over and destroyed the body's immune system; and such control of viral replication would be immensely helpful if it could be achieved. Indeed, the notion of a CTL-based HIV vaccine is surprisingly popular in view of the technical difficulties of producing it. David Garber and Mark Feinberg, respected HIV investigators at the Emory Vaccine Research Center in Atlanta, write:

> If widely implemented, such vaccines may have a significant impact on improving the quality and length of life for HIV-infected individuals, while at the same time reducing the rate at which HIV continues to spread throughout the human population.

But despite the importance of these T-cell responses against HIV, especially in the acute phase of infection, they ultimately fail to control HIV's effects. Nobody knows exactly why. It is clear that a CTL-based HIV vaccine would have to improve upon the immune response that is induced by natural infection. This is a huge demand to put on a vaccine and it is far from clear that it could be achieved. Vaccines of this kind would face the additional problem of overcoming HIV's remarkable genetic diversity.

The sum total of our knowledge about the genetics, biology, and geographical distribution of HIV indicates that vaccine scientists may have met their match in this adaptable foe. The reality seems to be that a vaccine against AIDS is becoming little more than a pipe dream.

> *"The majority of persons who are aware of their HIV infections substantially reduce sexual behaviors that might transmit HIV."*

Widespread Routine HIV Testing Is Needed to Control the Spread of AIDS

Bernard Branson, et al.

In September 2006 the federal Centers for Disease Control and Prevention (CDC) significantly expanded its HIV testing guidelines to recommend routine screening of all adults and all adolescents, ages thirteen to sixty-four, in all health-care settings. Previous CDC recommendations had focused on HIV testing of hospital patients and pregnant women. In the following viewpoint, CDC HIV/AIDS prevention coordinator Bernard M. Branson and colleagues explain why universal HIV screening is warranted to slow the spread of AIDS: Many people infected with HIV visit doctor's offices, STD clinics, and hospitals years before receiving a diagnosis, missing opportunities to begin early treatment; and increasing numbers of infected persons are younger

Bernard Branson, et al, "Revised Recommendations for HIV Testing of Adults, Adolescents and Pregnant Women in Health-Care Settings," *CDC-MMWR*, vol. 55, September 22, 2006, pp. 1–17. Information obtained from the Center for Disease Control (www.cdc.gov).

than twenty years old or heterosexual men and women unaware that they are at risk for HIV. The CDC argues that routine HIV screening that remains voluntary will save lives and health-care costs.

As you read, consider the following questions:

1. What four criteria that justify screening does HIV infection meet, according to the CDC recommendations?
2. What four benefits of routine HIV testing do the authors identify?
3. What recommendations does the CDC make concerning parental consent in HIV screening of adolescents?

Revised CDC [Centers for Disease Control and Prevention] recommendations advocate routine voluntary HIV screening as a normal part of medical practice, similar to screening for other treatable conditions. Screening is a basic public health tool used to identify unrecognized health conditions so treatment can be offered before symptoms develop and, for communicable diseases, so interventions can be implemented to reduce the likelihood of continued transmission.

HIV infection is consistent with all generally accepted criteria that justify screening: 1) HIV infection is a serious health disorder that can be diagnosed before symptoms develop; 2) HIV can be detected by reliable, inexpensive, and noninvasive screening tests; 3) infected patients have years of life to gain if treatment is initiated early, before symptoms develop; and 4) the costs of screening are reasonable in relation to the anticipated benefits. Among pregnant women, screening has proven substantially more effective than risk-based testing for detecting unsuspected maternal HIV infection and preventing perinatal transmission.

Rationale for New Recommendations

Often, persons with HIV infection visit health-care settings (e.g., hospitals, acute-care clinics, and sexually transmitted disease [STD] clinics) years before receiving a diagnosis but are not tested for HIV. Since the 1980s, the demographics of the HIV/AIDS epidemic in the United States have changed; increasing proportions of infected persons are aged <20 years, women, members of racial or ethnic minority populations, persons who reside outside metropolitan areas, and heterosexual men and women who frequently are unaware that they are at risk for HIV. As a result, the effectiveness of using risk-based testing [targeting only high-risk groups such as IV drug users] to identify HIV-infected persons has diminished.

Prevention strategies that incorporate universal HIV screening have been highly effective. For example, screening blood donors for HIV has nearly eliminated transfusion-associated HIV infection in the United States. In addition, incidence of pediatric HIV/AIDS in the United States has declined substantially since the 1990s, when prevention strategies began to include specific recommendations for routine HIV testing of pregnant women. Perinatal transmission rates can be reduced to <2% with universal screening of pregnant women in combination with prophylactic administration of antiretroviral drugs, scheduled cesarean delivery when indicated, and avoidance of breast feeding.

These successes contrast with a relative lack of progress in preventing sexual transmission of HIV, for which screening rarely is performed. Declines in HIV incidence observed in the early 1990s have leveled and might even have reversed in certain populations in recent years. Since 1998, the estimated number of new infections has remained stable at approximately 40,000 annually. In 2001, the Institute of Medicine (IOM) emphasized prevention services for HIV-infected persons and recommended policies for diagnosing H1V infections earlier to increase the number of HIV-infected persons who were aware of their infections and who were offered clinical and prevention services. The majority of persons who are aware of their HIV infections substantially reduce sexual

> # HIV Testing: A Cost-Effective Strategy
>
> In terms of money spent in testing versus money saved in health care and other costs, one-time HIV testing [compares] favorably to such routine health interventions as regular mammograms, colon cancer screening, or routine high blood pressure testing. . . .
>
> If HIV testing became universal, increased detection and heightened awareness might even cause the epidemic to finally subside, at least in affluent countries like the United States.
>
> *E. J. Mundell, "Wider HIV Testing Would Save Lives, Dollars,"*
> HealingWell.com, *February 9, 2005.*

behaviors that might transmit HIV after they become aware they are infected. In a meta-analysis of findings from eight studies, the prevalence of unprotected anal or vaginal intercourse with uninfected partners was on average 68% lower for HIV-infected persons who were aware of their status than it was for HIV-infected persons who were unaware of their status. To increase diagnosis of HIV infection, destigmatize the testing process, link clinical care with prevention, and ensure immediate access to clinical care for persons with newly identified HIV infection, IOM and other health-care professionals with expertise have encouraged adoption of routine HIV testing in all health-care settings. . . .

Recommendations for Adults and Adolescents

CDC recommends that diagnostic HIV testing and opt-out HIV screening be a part of routine clinical care in all health-care settings while also preserving the patient's option to decline HIV testing and ensuring a provider-patient relationship conducive to optimal clinical and preventive care. The recommendations are intended for providers in all health-care settings, including hospital EDs [emergency departments], urgent-care clinics, inpatient services, STD clinics or other venues offering clinical STD services, tuberculosis (TB) clinics, substance abuse treatment clinics, other public health clinics, community clinics, correctional health-care facilities, and primary care settings. The guidelines address HIV testing in health-care settings only; they do not modify existing guidelines concerning HIV counseling, testing, and referral for persons at high risk for HIV who seek or receive HIV testing in nonclinical settings (e.g., community-based organizations, outreach settings, or mobile vans).

Screening for HIV Infection:

- In all health-care settings, screening for HIV infection should be performed routinely for all patients aged 13–64 years. Health-care providers should initiate screening unless prevalence of undiagnosed HIV infection in their patients has been documented to be <0.1%. In the absence of existing data for HIV prevalence, health-care providers should initiate voluntary HIV screening until they establish that the diagnostic yield is <1 per 1,000 patients screened, at which point such screening is no longer warranted.

- All patients initiating treatment for TB should be screened routinely for HIV infection.

- All patients seeking treatment for STDs, including all patients attending STD clinics, should be screened routinely for HIV during each visit for a new complaint, regardless of whether the patient is known or suspected to have specific behavior risks for HIV infection.

Repeat Screening:

- Health-care providers should subsequently test all persons likely to be at high risk for HIV at least annually.

Persons likely to be at high risk include injection-drug users and their sex partners, persons who exchange sex for money or drugs, sex partners of HIV-infected persons, and MSM [men who have sex with men] or heterosexual persons who themselves or whose sex partners have had more than one sex partner since their most recent HIV test.

- Health-care providers should encourage patients and their prospective sex partners to be tested before initiating a new sexual relationship.

- Repeat screening of persons not likely to be at high risk for HIV should be performed on the basis of clinical judgment.

- Unless recent HIV test results are immediately available, any person whose blood or body fluid is the source of an occupational exposure for a health-care provider should be informed of the incident and tested for HIV infection at the time the exposure occurs.

Consent and Pretest Information:

- Screening should be voluntary and undertaken only with the patient's knowledge and understanding that HIV testing is planned.

- Patients should be informed orally or in writing that HIV testing will be performed unless they decline (opt-out screening). Oral or written information should include an explanation of HIV infection and the meanings of positive and negative test results, and the patient should be offered an opportunity to ask questions and to decline testing. With such notification, consent for HIV screening should be incorporated into the patient's general informed consent for medical care on the same basis as are other screening or diagnostic tests; a separate consent form for HIV testing is not recommended.

- Easily understood informational materials should be made available in the languages of the commonly encountered populations within the service area. The competence of interpreters and bilingual staff to provide language assistance to patients with limited English proficiency must be ensured.

- If a patient declines an HIV test, this decision should be documented in the medical record. . . .

Recommendations for Pregnant Women

These guidelines reiterate the recommendation for universal HIV screening early in pregnancy but advise simplifying the screening process to maximize opportunities for women to learn their HIV status during pregnancy, preserving the woman's option to decline HIV testing, and ensuring a provider-patient relationship conducive to optimal clinical and preventive care. All women should receive HIV screening consistent with the recommendations for adults and adolescents. HIV screening should be a routine component of preconception care, maximizing opportunities for all women to know their HIV status before conception. In addition, screening early in pregnancy enables HIV-infected women and their infants to benefit from appropriate and timely interventions (e.g., antiretroviral medications, scheduled cesarean delivery, and avoidance of breastfeeding). These recommendations are intended for clinicians who provide care to pregnant women and newborns and for health policy makers who have responsibility for these populations. . . .

Special Considerations for Screening Adolescents

Although parental involvement in an adolescent's health care is usually desirable, it typically is not required when the adolescent consents to HIV testing. However, laws concerning consent and confidentiality for HIV care differ among states.

Public health statutes and legal precedents allow for evaluation and treatment of minors for STDs without parental knowledge or consent, but not every state has defined HIV infection explicitly as a condition for which testing or treatment may proceed without parental consent. Health-care providers should endeavor to respect an adolescent's request for privacy. HIV screening should be discussed with all adolescents and encouraged for those who are sexually active. Providing information regarding HIV infection, HIV testing, HIV transmission, and implications of infection should be regarded as an essential component of the anticipatory guidance provided to all adolescents as part of primary care.

"In the absence of fully accessible HIV care [and] treatment ... federal efforts to expand HIV testing promotion will ultimately fail."

HIV Testing Alone Is Ineffective and Violates Individual Rights

Community HIV/AIDS Mobilization Project

In September 2006 the Centers for Disease Control and Prevention (CDC) issued new guidelines recommending voluntary, routine HIV testing for all people ages thirteen to sixty-four in all health-care settings. The following viewpoint is a formal statement of objections to the CDC guidelines, issued by the Community HIV/AIDS Mobilization Project (CHAMP) and endorsed by thirty-four local, state, and national AIDS and civil rights organizations. CHAMP argues that under the new guidelines people will be tested without fully understanding what they are consenting to; HIV-negative people will not get much-needed counseling; and testing will do HIV-positive people little good if they do not have access to treatment. CHAMP, based in New York City, supports community activism in intersecting issues of AIDS, social and economic justice, and civil rights.

Community HIV/AIDS Mobilization Project, "Federal HIV Testing Initiatives Can Only Succeed with Expanded Healthcare, Patient, and Provider Education," *CHAMP Policy Statement*, September 21, 2006. Reproduced by permission.

As you read, consider the following questions:

1. According to CHAMP, why is HIV testing under the new CDC guidelines not truly voluntary?

2. In what ways does the author say even people who receive HIV-negative test results will be badly served by the expanded CDC screening recommendations?

3. What important stakeholder groups were not allowed to comment on or contribute to the CDC's HIV testing guidelines, according to CHAMP?

In response to new guidelines by the U.S. Centers for Disease Control and Prevention (CDC) on HIV testing in healthcare settings:

We Support the Routine Offer of HIV Testing

Expanding the offer of voluntary HIV counseling and testing services in healthcare settings is good public health policy. Routinely offered HIV testing will help reach more individuals who may be unaware of their HIV-positive status as well as those who are HIV-negative but engaging in high-risk behaviors. Encouraging individuals to learn their status will help slow the spread of HIV and assist those who are HIV-positive live healthier, longer lives.

We Support CDC's Recommendation that HIV Testing Remain Voluntary and Free of Coercion

Mandated or coercive testing strategies threaten to alienate people with or at risk for HIV—the very individuals whose involvement is pivotal to successful efforts against the epidemic. By merely encouraging testing, and ensuring it is readily available and properly explained, most people will recognize its benefits and accept testing on their own volition. The new CDC guidelines' recommendation of reliance on a patient's general consent to medical services without a requirement to document the offering of the test and the right of the patient to refuse without penalty does not, especially in the context of hectic and understaffed clinics and emergency rooms, constitute voluntary, consensual testing. Nonconsensual testing violates individuals' basic human rights to consent to their own medical procedures.

We Strongly Disagree with CDC Recommendations to Eliminate Pre-test Counseling and Informed, Written Consent to Testing

An expanded focus on testing without counseling and written, informed consent will put people at risk for testing without their prior knowledge or approval—a clear violation of medical ethics and human rights.

De-linking counseling from testing is also highly problematic for many vulnerable populations. For example, adolescents and young people, who are at particularly high risk of stigma and rejection from family and friends when disclosing their HIV status and who are often dependent on adults to access health care services and reimbursement, may not be fully prepared for the consequences of an HIV diagnosis in the absence of counseling and written, informed consent.

Pre-test counseling and informed, written consent to testing open conversations about HIV/AIDS between patients and providers and help dispel commonly held myths that perpetuate high-risk behaviors and stigmatizing attitudes. Open and honest communication about HIV/AIDS and the behaviors that can (and cannot) transmit HIV are instrumental to progress against the epidemic. Accurate education about HIV/AIDS must be expanded on a scale equal to or greater than the expansion of HIV testing.

We Support Efforts to Develop
New, Innovative Strategies to Expedite
Counseling and Informed Written
Consent to HIV Testing

We urge CDC to develop, pilot, and disseminate new models that offer clients much briefer means to receive context-appropriate HIV counseling in various settings. We also support the development of innovative ways to speed the attainment of written informed consent to testing. Testing conducted without these important components, however, will forgo critically important opportunities to educate at-risk individuals about HIV prevention. Several of the undersigned organizations have examples of such initiatives in use across the country and urge CDC to use the opportunity to learn about and implement our best practices.

We Call on CDC to Address the
Needs of HIV-negative Individuals at
High Risk of Infection and People
Without Regular Access to Healthcare

We are gravely concerned that high-risk HIV-negative individuals will fail to receive the education and support they need to remain HIV-free under testing procedures that exclude counseling and informed written consent. Without any counseling or attempts to link people into risk-reduction services, these high-risk negatives may be misled into falsely believing that a negative test result means that they are not at risk for HIV, thereby increasing their risk. The fact that not all populations with high rates of undetected HIV will encounter a clinical setting where they may be offered an HIV test must also be taken into consideration in attempts to reduce racial disparities in early diagnosis of HIV, and strategies to reach them must be adequately promoted and funded.

Good Versus Bad
HIV Testing Programs

Human Rights Watch pointed to a program in Uganda that provides treatment, counseling, condoms, and voluntary HIV testing in people's homes that has decreased HIV transmission by 98 percent. By contrast, research by Human Rights Watch in the Dominican Republic, Romania, and Zimbabwe found that HIV testing practices that were not voluntary, were not linked to counseling and care, and failed to protect confidentiality effectively discouraged people from seeking necessary care and led to increased stigma and abuse.

Human Rights Watch, "AIDS Conference:
Drive for HIV Testing Must Respect Rights," August 10, 2006.

We Strongly Object to the Limited Degree of Input Solicited from Community Stakeholders in the Development of These Guidelines and the Secrecy with Which CDC Advanced and Finalized Them

In March 2006, CDC developed and quietly circulated a draft of its revised HIV testing guidelines, sidestepping the typical public posting process in the *Federal Register* that generally allows 60 or more days for public comment. Instead, CDC sent its draft revised guidelines to a select group of individuals and allowed just 15 working days for the selected interested parties to register their opinions. While CDC did solicit input from clinicians and other medical providers, we believe efforts to involve people living with HIV, community advocates, social workers, outreach workers, local administrators of HIV services, and other workers responsible for conducting HIV testing were wholly insufficient. CDC has demonstrated a pattern of secrecy and poor engagement of stakeholders in regards to HIV prevention policy. Reviving our nation's lagging HIV prevention efforts will require new, collaborative relationships that engage and involve AIDS community members.

We Call on CDC to Involve Greater Numbers of People Living with HIV, Community Stakeholders, and Clinicians in Efforts to Strengthen HIV Testing Promotion and Acceptance in the U.S.

We agree that testing modalities can and should be improved to account for changes in technology, the growth and diversity of the epidemic, and the need to reach more people with HIV testing, prevention, and care services. We also believe CDC should take a leadership role in developing and widely disseminating proven models to deliver voluntary HIV counseling and testing services in ways that expedite counseling and the attainment of informed, written consent to testing. Federal initiatives to expand the offer of HIV testing, however, must be guided and informed by the experiences of people living with HIV/AIDS, community-based organizations, and HIV clinicians who are at the forefront of the fight against the epidemic.

We Believe that the Effects and Impact of Routine Offering of HIV Tests in Healthcare Settings Must be Carefully Documented and Analyzed

The effectiveness, costs, barriers, correlates of relative success and possible unintended consequences of these guidelines must be documented and characterized in whatever form these recommendations are promoted and implemented. Key questions must be answered, such as how many new cases of infection are diagnosed in this way compared to other strategies, what proportion of people with newly recognized HIV are successfully linked to ongoing care and which populations are most receptive to routinely offered screening tests. The CDC must call for adequately funded operation research to track and report on the outcome and impact of these recommended practices both in themselves and as compared to alternate uses of the same resources.

We Believe Testing Promotion Alone Will Not Reverse the Escalation of HIV/AIDS in the U.S.

In the absence of fully accessible HIV care, treatment, and support services, and a more robust HIV prevention agenda, federal efforts to expand HIV testing promotion will ultimately fail at decreasing HIV-related morbidity, mortality, and new infections. The federal government must match its support for HIV testing with proven prevention and care strategies to adequately address the size and complexity of HIV/AIDS in the U.S. today. All testing, prevention, and care measures also must include targeted approaches to meet the needs of those at greatest risk of infection and transmission, as well as those at risk of not seeking care once diagnosed.

We Believe Funding for New Testing Initiatives Should be in Addition to Existing Program Funding

Expanding support for the routine offer of HIV testing should not shift funds away from more targeted, community-based testing or HIV prevention programs. Indeed, Congress must appropriate a minimum $1 billion annually for HIV prevention programs in order to begin to reduce the number of new HIV infections that occur annually in the U.S. In addition, the CDC should make clear that it expects the costs of offering routine HIV testing and counseling in healthcare settings to be borne by insurers and other payers already covering the costs of the care being sought.

> "As the only 100-percent-effective way to prevent sexual transmission of HIV, the practice of abstinence until marriage needs to be a key message."

Abstinence-Based AIDS Prevention Programs Effectively Stem the Spread of AIDS

U.S. Agency for International Development

In 2003 President George W. Bush announced the President's Emergency Plan for AIDS Relief (PEPFAR), a five-year, $15 billion, multifaceted plan for combating HIV/AIDS around the world. One of its key prevention strategies is an abstinence-until-marriage program targeted at young people ages ten to twenty-four. In the following viewpoint, the U.S. Agency for International Development (USAID) explains the benefits of PEPFAR's abstinence-focused program, which USAID implements through mostly faith-based organizations in Africa and the Caribbean. USAID is an independent federal agency founded in 1961 to provide economic and humanitarian assistance worldwide.

U.S. Agency for International Development, "Healthy Choices for Youth," October 2005.

As you read, consider the following questions:

1. What percentage of new HIV infections occurs in the fifteen-to-twenty-four-year-old age group, as reported by USAID?

2. What three behaviors in addition to abstinence-until-marriage does USAID's *Abstinence and Behavior Change for Youth* program promote?

3. In how many African countries is PEPFAR's abstinence-based program conducted, according to USAID? In which African country is most activity concentrated?

As the only 100-percent-effective way to prevent sexual transmission of HIV, the practice of abstinence until marriage needs to be a key message, especially to youth. Pairing abstinence education with messages about the future and the importance of monogamy is crucial since half of all new infections occur in the 15–24 age group, and multiple concurrent sexual partnerships are the main driver of generalized epidemics.

In 2004, USAID announced $100 million in new grants under the *Abstinence and Behavior Change for Youth* program. This initiative will expand activities in support of abstinence until marriage, fidelity in marriage, monogamous relationships, and avoidance of unhealthy sexual behaviors among youth aged 10 to 24. The initiative recognizes the important role that parents, families, community- and faith-based groups, and other key leadership within all sectors play in positively supporting healthy choices for youth.

USAID Partners in Africa and the Caribbean

The **Adventist Development and Relief Agency** (ADRA) provides community development and disaster relief in more than 120 countries worldwide. As part of the Emergency Plan, the *Abstinence and Behavioral Change for Youth* program will expand ADRA's current activities in Kenya and Tanzania, reaching more than one million youth aged 10 to 24 with abstinence and fidelity messages by September 2009.

The **American Red Cross** (ARC) works with a global network to bring emergency relief and improved living conditions to vulnerable people in Eastern Europe, Africa, Asia, the Pacific, the Americas, and the former Soviet Union. As part of the Emergency Plan, ARC's *Together We Can* project will scale up proven HIV/AIDS peer-education methodology for youth in Tanzania, Haiti, and Guyana. Through an interactive eight-hour curriculum, together with culturally appropriate community-mobilization approaches, the program will reach 766,000 youth to encourage delayed sexual activity, secondary abstinence, and safer behaviors. ARC will also build the capacity of national Red Cross societies and selected local branches to implement effective youth HIV-prevention programs.

Catholic Relief Services (CRS) serves the poor in 99 countries on five continents through programs in emergency relief, HIV/AIDS, health, agriculture, education, microfinance, and peace building. As part of the Emergency Plan, CRS' *Avoiding Risk, Affirming Life* project will work with faith- and community-based partners in Ethiopia, Rwanda, and Uganda to encourage abstinence until marriage, secondary abstinence, and fidelity in marriage. Drawing upon extensive prevention experience in more than 30 countries, CRS will enable a robust, locally driven response, including parishes, parents, caregivers, church leaders, women's groups, and youth clubs. While youth will be the focus, adults (especially older males) will also be targeted with messages of fidelity and sexual responsibility as a means to protect vulnerable youth. The project will directly reach 957,125 youth and 395,360 adults with interactive messages on abstinence and mutual fidelity.

Food for the Hungry helps some of the world's most disadvantaged people in 47 countries through child-development programs, agriculture and clean-water projects, health and nutrition programs, education, micro-enterprise loans, and emergency relief. As part of the Emergency Plan, Food for the Hungry collaborates with eight other Association of Evangelical Relief and Development Organizations under the *Healthy Choices Leading to Life* project. This program aims to empower churches, schools, and other community-based organizations to provide youth and adult stakeholders with the skills, information, and strengthened community-level social structures necessary to reduce HIV transmission and risky behaviors among targeted youth and adults in Ethiopia, Haiti, Mozambique, and Nigeria. The five-year project will build upon existing faith-based networks to reach more than 1,389,000 youth and children and 243,800 influential adults via direct contact, and an additional 55 million people through television and radio messages.

FreshMinistries is an ecumenical, faith-based nonprofit organization working to improve people's lives and to bring hope to those living in distressed conditions. As part of the Emergency Plan, the Anglican Church (as represented by FreshMinistries), the Church of the Province of South Africa, the Episcopal Diocese of Washington, and other partners are implementing *SIYAFUNDISA* ("Teaching Our Children"), a five-year project to reduce HIV/AIDS incidence by promoting abstinence and fidelity in South Africa, Mozambique, and Namibia. The program will be implemented through 100 parishes in the first year. Approximately 132 parishes will be added annually, serving approximately 150,000 youth and 50,000 adults each year.

HOPE worldwide is a nonprofit, faith-based charity that provides education, medical services, and programs for disadvantaged children and the elderly in 75 countries. As part of the Emergency Plan, *HOPE worldwide* seeks to enhance local HIV/AIDS prevention through abstinence, faithfulness, and the reduction of harmful sexual behavior for youth and other groups. Community action teams include parents, teachers, and learners who develop local strategies to reinforce behavior change among the youth. The project aims to promote abstinence and behavior change among 592,480 youth and parents in Botswana, Côte D'lvoire, Kenya, Nigeria, and South Africa, and will be carried out in schools, churches, youth groups, sports clubs, and other faith-based organizations.

The **International Youth Foundation** (IYF) works in nearly 70 countries to improve the conditions and prospects for young people. As part of the Emergency Plan, IYF's *Support to HIV/AIDS Prevention through Abstinence and Behavior Change for Youth* program will work through the *Empowering Africa's Young People Initiative*, which involves 16 indigenous sub-grantees in Tanzania, Uganda, and Zambia. Interventions will reach more than 500,000 youth and 200,000 adults to change knowledge, attitudes, and behaviors toward abstinence and faithfulness. IYF will focus on four strategic objectives and will aim to address the crosscutting themes of gender, youth participation, local capacity building, local ownership, and sustainability.

Pact is a networked organization that builds the capacity of local leaders and organizations to meet pressing social needs in dozens of countries around the world. As part of the Emergency Plan, Pact will implement the *Youth and Children with Health Options Involving Community Engagement Strategies (Y-CHOICES)* program. Focusing on community involvement in helping children and youth make educated choices about behaviors that affect their health, *Y-CHOICES* will provide youth, their families, and their communities with improved information, services, and skills supportive of lifestyle choices and behavior change. In Ethiopia, Pact aims to bring abstinence and faithfulness messages to more than 700,000 secondary students. In Zambia, Pact will work with 66 local partner organizations to develop age-appropriate information, education, communication, and behavior-change-communication materials on abstinence and fidelity that address risk factors directly relevant to Zambian youth, especially young girls.

Abstinence-Until-Marriage Programs in the United States

For about two decades, the top public health agencies in America urged young people to use condoms to reduce the risk of HIV/AIDS and other sexually transmitted diseases.

But the U.S. government has dramatically reversed course. Over the past five years, it has spent nearly $1 billion to persuade young people that the only safe form of sex is within marriage—and that condoms are not as effective as people think. . . .

As recently as 1988, just one in 50 junior and senior high schools taught abstinence-only-until-marriage programs. [In 2005] those programs are in about one-third of schools in the United States, reaching some eight million students.

Ed Bradley, "Taking the Pledge," 60 Minutes, September 18, 2005.

PATH collaborates with diverse public- and private-sector partners to provide appropriate health technologies and to create sustainable, culturally relevant solutions, enabling communities worldwide to break longstanding cycles of poor health. In support of the Emergency Plan, PATH's *Scouting for Solutions*—a strategic-skills- and dialogue-based project—will promote abstinence until marriage, fidelity, monogamous relationships, and avoidance of unhealthy sexual behaviors among Scouts in Kenya and Uganda. In partnership with national Scouts Associations, PATH will reach an estimated 400,000 girls and boys aged 12 to 15 years with intensive and repeated messages and activities. By building on Scouts Associations' existing structures and programs, the project will quickly and effectively scale up state-of-the-art HIV education for these youth, their families, and their communities.

Salesian Missions provides education and technical training for impoverished children and youth in more than 128 countries. Salesians carry out activities in many countries that have profoundly experienced the impact by HIV/AIDS, with a focus on training vulnerable and at-risk youth to take care of their health through abstinence, fidelity, and addressing harmful gender norms. In support of the Emergency Plan, Salesian Missions will implement the *LIFE CHOICES* program at existing Salesian youth centers, schools, parish outreach facilities, centers for orphans and vulnerable children, and community/social outreach programs in Kenya, Tanzania, and South Africa. The project aims to reach 169,000 youth.

Samaritan's Purse seeks to meet the needs of victims of war, poverty, natural disasters, disease, and famine. Its *There is Hope* project will mobilize, equip, and train older youth and Christian grassroots youth leaders who work with youth to educate them and to prevent new HIV infection. The program aims to mobilize, equip, and train older youth, pastors, women, and youth leaders to speak truthfully without increasing HIV/AIDS stigma to youth, and to care for these youth by mentoring them and involving them in community service to vulnerable households. The project plans to work in more than 480 communities in Mozambique, Kenya, Uganda, and Ethiopia, and to reach more than one million youth, youth leaders, and parents with awareness messages, home-based-care training, micromedia campaigns, mentoring, and/or a life-skills and character-based education.

World Relief works in 24 nations on four continents equipping communities and churches to help victims of poverty, disease, hunger, war, disasters, and persecution. As part of the Emergency Plan, World Relief's five-year *Mobilizing Youth for Life* project will scale up well-established HIV-prevention activities for youth in Haiti, Kenya, Mozambique, and Rwanda, encouraging abstinence until marriage, fidelity in marriage, and everyday healthy choices. Working through partnerships with 8,000 churches and 4,800 schools and community organizations, World Relief plans to reach more than 1.8 million youth, 15,000 volunteers and peer mentors, 16,500 pastors and teachers, and 70,000 parents. World Relief will also help to establish 1,750 youth clubs to provide continued social support.

World Vision is a Christian relief and development organization dedicated to the well-being of all people, especially children, through emergency relief, education, health care, economic development, and promotion of justice. In partnership with the Johns Hopkins Bloomberg School of Public Health Center for Communication Programs, World Vision's *Abstinence and Risk Avoidance for Youth* (ARK) project will combine the reach and power of the faith community with the weight of proven public-health and communication methodologies. The project will be implemented in Haiti, Kenya, and Tanzania through four faith-based organization partners, a national and a regional civil society network, and a training institute. ARK aims to encourage behavior—primarily abstinence and mutual monogamy—that will reduce risk among youth of becoming infected with HIV, with a focus on creating supportive family and community environments. It will also have programs to help sexually active youth reduce risk. A predominant theme will be to create behavior change through small groups and peer support, and to link abstinence and fidelity intervention activities to a continuum of care where available.

| "*Abstinence-only programs in fact increase HIV risk.*"

Abstinence-Based AIDS Prevention Programs Fail to Halt the Global Epidemic

Jonathan Cohen and Tony Tate

In the following viewpoint, Jonathan Cohen and Tony Tate argue that abstinence-focused programs such as those implemented by USAID in Uganda to reduce HIV transmission have little to no impact on people's sexual behavior in the short term, and are actually harmful in the long term because they make people less likely to use contraceptives, and thus more likely to contract and transmit HIV once they become sexually active. Jonathan Cohen is a researcher in the HIV/AIDS and Human Rights Program of Human Rights Watch, an independent nongovernmental organization, based in New York, dedicated to investigating and exposing human rights abuses worldwide. Tony Tate is a researcher in the Children's Rights Division of Human Rights Watch.

Jonathon Cohen and Tony Tate, "The Less They Know, the Better," *Human Rights Watch*, vol. 17, March 2005. Copyright © 2005 *Human Rights Watch*. Reproduced by permission.

As you read, consider the following questions:

1. What evidence do the authors give to support their claim that abstinence-only programs do not change people's sexual attitudes and behaviors?

2. According to Cohen and Tate, what alternatives to abstinence-only programs do reduce high-risk sexual activity?

3. What evidence of HIV incidence in Africa do the authors use to dispute U.S. government claims that delaying first sexual intercourse by even a year can have significant impact on the AIDS epidemic?

Encouraging young people to delay sex and reduce the number of their sex partners forms a rational part of any comprehensive approach to HIV prevention. However, governments have an obligation not to censor or distort information about effective methods of HIV prevention, including condoms, and to pursue HIV prevention strategies that are scientifically valid. When moral considerations (such as discouraging sex for its own sake or promoting the institution of marriage) overwhelm sound HIV prevention, this impedes the realization of internationally recognized human rights, including the right to information, the right to the highest attainable standard of health, and ultimately the right to life. . . .

Abstinence-Only Programs Don't Work

The exportation of abstinence-only programs from the United States to Uganda [and other African countries] is occurring notwithstanding unrefuted evidence of the ineffectiveness and potential harms of these programs. Government-funded evaluations in at least twelve U.S. states, as well as a federally mandated independent evaluation authorized in 1997, indicate that abstinence-until-marriage programs show no long-term success in delaying sexual initiation or reducing sexual risk-taking behaviors among program participants, and that program participants are less likely to use contraceptives once they become sexually active. The Institute of Medicine, a body of experts that acts under a Congressional charter as an advisor to the U.S. federal government, noted in 2001 that there was no evidence supporting abstinence-only programs, and that investing "millions of dollars of federal ... funds ... in abstinence-only programs with no evidence of effectiveness constitutes poor fiscal and health policy." Assessments such as these provide some indication of the likely success (or failure) of abstinence-only programs in Uganda, as U.S.-based abstinence-only programs are administered according to the same guidelines, and in some cases by the same organizations, as proposed Ugandan programs. No independent evaluations of abstinence-only programs exist from Uganda, largely because such programs did not exist there on a significant scale before 2004.

Evaluations of abstinence-only programs typically measure whether program participants change their sexual attitudes, intentions, and behaviors over the short and long term. According to a 2004 review of abstinence-only program evaluations conducted by Washington, D.C.-based Advocates for Youth, only one program showed any impact on participants' sexual behavior, and this impact disappeared by the end of the program. While some programs had short-term impact on participants' attitudes and intentions to abstain, and one (in Pennsylvania) had some long-term impact on intentions, these attitudes and intentions did not translate into behavior changes. In one county in Pennsylvania, 42 percent of female participants were sexually active by the second year of their abstinence-only program. In another, rates of sexual debut among females increased from 6 to 30 percent as program participants progressed from seventh to ninth grade. In Minnesota, where an abstinence program showed mixed results on changing attitudes towards abstinence in the long-term, the percentage of youths who were sexually active was higher in several counties with abstinence programs than the state average.

Abstinence-Only Programs Produce Ignorance of Contraception

Of equal concern is that abstinence-only programs may discourage young people from using contraception once they become sexually active. As noted above, abstinence-only programs do not provide participants with information about contraception other than (sometimes exaggerated) failure rates. . . .

Proponents of abstinence-only programs often claim that teaching young people about condoms and safer sex will contradict or otherwise undermine the message of abstinence. However, studies that compare abstinence-only education with programs that include factual information about contraception show the latter to be more effective on all counts. A 2001 report analyzing studies of HIV prevention programs found that programs that include information about both abstinence and condoms can delay the onset of sex and increase condom use among sexually active teens. The same study found no evidence existed that abstinence-only programs had an effect on sexual behavior. A 1998 study comparing a program that educated students about safer sex (including condom use) with an abstinence-only program found that both programs affected sexual behavior in the short term, but that the safer sex program was more effective at reducing unprotected sexual intercourse and frequency of intercourse in the long term.

In 2001, the Institute of Medicine concluded that scientific studies have shown that comprehensive sex and HIV/AIDS education programs and condom availability programs can be effective in reducing high-risk sexual behaviors. A 1997 report by the Joint United Nations Programme on HIV/AIDS (UNAIDS) found evidence that sexual health education for

Abstinence-Only Programs Have Wiped Out Uganda's Success Against HIV

While PEPFAR [President's Emergency Plan for AIDS Relief] has jeopardized AIDS programs in a multitude of countries, the Ugandan case has been especially tragic. During the 1990s, the country was seen as a poster child for eradicating AIDS rates in Africa, consistently hailed for its effective efforts in combating the global epidemic. At the cornerstone of its initiatives was a quality contraceptive program, which included a virtually unlimited supply of condoms, many of which were handed out for free at local bars to promote safe sex.

Yet in September 2006, data presented at the International AIDS Conference in Toronto confirmed that the tremendous gains Uganda made in the fight against HIV have withered away in the past five years—since [President George] Bush took the reins of U.S. policies. The cited reason? More unprotected sex, stemming mainly from a significant condom shortage that, according to Stephan Lewis, U.N. Special Envoy for HIV/AIDS in Africa, is a crisis "being driven and exacerbated by the extreme policies that the administration in the United States is now pursuing."

Adam Lichtenheld, "No-Condom Policy Leaves Ugandans at High Risk," Badger Herald (Madison, WI), September 21, 2006.

children and young people that included the promotion of condom use and safer sexual practices, did not increase participants' sexual activity.

In 2004, a "gold-standard" review of HIV prevention research by the Cochrane Collaborative Review Group on HIV infection and AIDS concluded that "[p]rograms promoting abstinence were found to be ineffective at increasing abstinent behavior and were possibly harmful; more rigorous research is needed to determine the effectiveness of abstinence programs on HIV risk." A 2004 consensus statement in the *Lancet*, signed by numerous experts in HIV prevention from around the world, stressed abstinence as a "first priority" for young people who are not sexually active but concluded:

> For those young people who are sexually active, correct and consistent condom use should be supported. Young people, and others should be informed that correct and consistent condom use lowers the risk of HIV (by about 80–90% for reported "always use") and of various sexually transmitted infections and pregnancy, and they should be cautioned about the consequences of inconsistent use.

Officials of the U.S. government did not endorse the *Lancet* statement, though they were asked to do so.

Abstinence-Only Programs Increase HIV Risk

U.S. officials systematically ignore independent evaluations of abstinence-only programs, instead making broad and unscientific claims about the benefits of abstinence. The U.S. global AIDS strategy, for example, posits that "[d]elaying first sexual intercourse by even a year can have significant impact on the health and well-being of adolescents and on the progress of the epidemic in communities." Beyond failing to cite evidence for this claim, the strategy neglects to mention that some countries with higher average ages of sexual debut than Uganda—Zimbabwe and South Africa, for example—have much higher rates of HIV incidence. The important point is that delaying sex does not protect people from HIV unless they protect themselves once they become sexually active. Abstinence-only programs in fact increase HIV risk by withholding information about contraception and safer sex and by suggesting that married people are safe from HIV infection.

As further "proof" of abstinence-only programs, proponents frequently cite evidence of reduced teen pregnancy rates in the United States in the 1980s and 1990s, a period that saw increased federal funding for abstinence-only programs. This logical fallacy assumes that just because abstinence-only programs occurred at the same time as a reduction in teen pregnancy, they must have caused this reduction. Indeed, studies also show that contraceptive use increased during the same period, and . . . that rates of premarital sex are higher in some regions with abstinence-only programs than in those without these programs. The fact that participants in abstinence-only programs are less likely to use contraception once they become sexually active suggests that teen pregnancy rates might have dropped even further were it not for these programs.

"The Vatican rejection of condoms ... helped the spread [of HIV/AIDS], especially in areas of the world where Catholic influence is high."

The Catholic Church Should Endorse Condom Use to Reduce HIV Infection

James Carroll

Writer and historian James Carroll was ordained to the Catholic priesthood in 1969 and served as Catholic chaplain of Boston University until leaving the priesthood in 1974. He is currently distinguished scholar-in-residence at Suffolk University in Boston and a contributor to the Boston Globe, *the* New Yorker, *and other periodicals on political and religious topics. In the following viewpoint, Carroll castigates the Catholic Church for not permitting condom use in the face of condoms' demonstrated effectiveness in preventing HIV infection. He is equally appalled by the Vatican's position that condoms actually promote the spread of HIV, and views the church as complicit in the death of millions. Carroll welcomes as long overdue a 2006 Vatican report that Pope Benedict XVI will be reconsidering its absolute position.*

As you read, consider the following questions:

1. How do Carroll's views of the Catholic tradition of ministry for people with HIV/AIDS and the Vatican's traditional prohibition of condom use differ?

2. According to the author, what potential change in the Vatican's position against condom use would be a step in the right direction?

3. How has the ban on condom use been catastrophic for the Catholic Church, in Carroll's opinion?

Caring for the sick has always been a defining act of religion, as if every conception of God must be measured by its generation of compassion. Among Catholics, the tradition of the "corporal works of mercy," associated with Jesus himself, long ago spawned a commitment to provide for the health of human beings, which led to the institutionalization of medical service. Catholic hospitals are the pride of the church. When I was a child, family illness prompted visits to Providence Hospital in Washington, and I remember the winged garb of the nursing sisters as a particular symbol of all that made life on this earth trustworthy.

Such associations form the backdrop of the shock it was when the Catholic Church failed in its response to the arrival of HIV/AIDS. Not that compassion was lacking. Catholic hospitals and other ministries threw themselves into caring for those who became infected, and today, across Europe, Africa, and the Americas, much of such care is provided in Catholic settings. But the urgent need for active prevention soon showed itself, and because the disease can be transmitted sexually, that required the advocacy of condom use.

In 1987 US Surgeon General C. Everett Koop recommended condoms for the prevention of the spread of HIV. One scientific study after another demonstrated the effectiveness of condoms in reducing risk of infection, yet centers of

Some Catholic Cardinals Favor Reform of the Condom Ban

The 1987 document *Donum Vitae*, which [Pope Benedict XVI] signed together with the late Pope [John Paul II], declared that the Roman Catholic Church could never agree to the use of contraceptives in homosexual relationships or by men and women who were not married. However, it omitted to mention married couples. In recent years, the case for condoms as a defence against AIDS has been taken up publicly by several Roman Catholic leaders. The Belgian cardinal Godfried Daneels broke the taboo in 2004 when he said it was morally different from using a condom for birth control.

The following year, the Pope's own theologian, Cardinal Georges Cottier, signalled doubts within the papal household and argued that the Roman Catholic "theology of life" could be used to justify a lifting of the ban. "The virus is transmitted during a sexual act; so at the same time as [bringing] life there is also a risk of transmitting death," he said. "And that is where the commandment 'thou shalt not kill' is valid."

Cardinal Carlo Maria Martini, a former archbishop of Milan who was considered a candidate for the papacy, said in [2006] that a married person with HIV was "obliged" to protect his or her partner from the disease.

John Hooper, "After Decades of Opposition, Vatican View on Condoms Begins to Shift," Guardian, November 23, 2000.

cultural conservatism resisted that message—none more consistently than the hierarchy of the Catholic Church.

"Although proven strategies exist to prevent new HIV infections," the UN declared in 2005, "essential prevention strategies reach only a fraction of those who need them." The Vatican has a special responsibility here, for it not only repeatedly rejected condom use for the sake of HIV prevention but argued—for example in its 2003 document "Family Values and Safe Sex"—that condoms, instead of inhibiting the spread of HIV/AIDS, promote it. This unconscionable denial was rooted in the most rigid of moral theologies, as if any loosening of Vatican condemnations of contraception—never mind that disease prevention differs from birth control—would lead to the collapse of Catholic authority.

The Vatican Bears Responsibility for the Spread of AIDS

In the years since Koop's advocacy of condoms, HIV/AIDS has continued to spread, so that by now more than 40 million people are infected, and the rates are going up (13,000 new infections each day). No Vatican policy could have stopped the spread of the disease, but there can be no doubt that Vatican rejection of condoms, and its aggressive campaign against condom use, helped that spread, especially in areas of the world where Catholic influence is high.

[In April 2006] came news reports that Pope Benedict XVI has ordered a Vatican reconsideration of its position on condoms and HIV/AIDS. "We are conducting a very profound scientific, technical, and moral study," said the head of the Vatican office for healthcare. The study may be restricted to condom use between married couples, one of whom carries the infection, but even a change in that limited context would be significant. Any mitigation of absolutism in Vatican rejection of condoms would be a welcome step in the right direction. Indeed, the announcement that a change is being considered is already a mitigation.

Yet as a Catholic I respond to this news with complicated feelings. It is one thing to toss out the doctrine of Limbo, say, or to drop regulations about abstaining from meat on Friday. The issue raised here is graver.

The consequences of this Catholic mistake have been catastrophic. Cultural prejudice against condoms, often widespread, has been reinforced. Women for whom condoms can be a crucial protection and a method of self-assertion have been kept at risk and disempowered. Priests, nuns, and the few bishops who denounced the condom ban have been disciplined. Catholic lay people who have been savvy enough to ignore it have been put in bad conscience. HIV/AIDS education has been equated with the promotion of promiscuity. Catholic leaders have falsely defined condoms as ineffective. Prevention of illness has been put in opposition to compassion for the sick. Homophobia has been sacralized. The Vatican's rigid adherence to this teaching in the face of monumental human suffering has been central to the broader collapse of Catholic moral authority.

But even these disasters pale beside the dominant fact of this tragedy: For more than 20 years, the hierarchy's rejection of condom use has been killing people. Even were the Vatican to change its position now—and pray it does—Catholics must still reckon with that betrayal.

| *"Condoms may even be one of the main reasons for the spread of HIV/AIDS."*

The Catholic Church Must Oppose Condom Use for HIV/AIDS Prevention

Alfonso Cardinal Lopez Trujillo

Alfonso Lopez Trujillo, a Colombian cardinal of the Roman Catholic Church since 1983, is president of the Holy See's Pontifical Council for the Family in Rome. In the following viewpoint, Lopez Trujillo defends the church's long-standing opposition to condom use for the prevention of HIV infection. He calls programs that advocate condom use gravely irresponsible because they convey the mistaken idea that condoms do protect against HIV and other sexually transmitted diseases, and they undermine the moral commitment to premarital abstinence and marital fidelity, which he argues are far more effective than condoms in reducing the spread of HIV/AIDS.

As you read, consider the following questions:

1. What scientific evidence does Lopez Trujillo present to support his argument that condoms do not protect against HIV infection?

Alfonso Cardinal Lopez Trujillo, "Family Values Versus Safe Sex," *Population Research Institute*, January–February 2004. Reproduced by permission.

2. How do condoms actually promote the spread of HIV/ AIDS, in the author's opinion?

3. According to Lopez Trujillo, why would the Catholic Church oppose condom use even if condoms were 100 percent effective against HIV and STDs?

The Catholic Church has repeatedly criticized programs promoting condoms as a totally effective and sufficient means of AIDS prevention. The different Bishops' Conferences all over the world have expressed their concern regarding this problem. The Catholic Bishops of South Africa, Botswana and Swaziland categorically "regard the widespread and indiscriminate promotion of condoms as an immoral and misguided weapon in our battle against HIV/AIDS for the following reasons:

- The use of condoms goes against human dignity.

- Condoms change the beautiful act of love into a selfish search for pleasure—while rejecting responsibility.

- Condoms do not guarantee protection against HIV/ AIDS.

- Condoms may even be one of the main reasons for the spread of HIV/AIDS. Apart from the possibility of condoms being faulty or wrongly used, they contribute to the breaking down of self-control and mutual respect."

The Sub-commission for Family and Life of the Spanish Episcopal Conference said that the campaigns that promote the condom in Spain to supposedly stop HIV/AIDS are gravely irresponsible for three reasons: "because they tend to be deceitful, because they hide information, and because they do not contribute towards prevention, but rather to a greater spread of risky behavior."

The Catholic Bishops' Conference of the Philippines maintained that "[t]he moral dimension of the problem of HIV-

Some Catholic Cardinals Strongly Oppose Reform of the Ban on Condoms

One of the biggest challenges the Catholic Church is facing is how to deal with mounting pressure for the promotion of condom use. Early in 2005 British International Development Secretary Clare Short took a swipe at the Church for its opposition to condom use in Africa. "The Catholic Church is stuck and wrong on these questions," she said. The Senegal SECAM Conference, on the other hand, made it clear that the Church would only fight the disease using methods that adhere to the Church's teachings.

"Using condoms as a means of preventing AIDS can only lead to sexual promiscuity," says Archbishop Dominic Bulamatari of the Democratic Republic of the Congo, who attended the conference.

Some political leaders are also questioning the wisdom of promoting condoms. [In 2004], Ugandan President Yoweri Museveni accused the West of promoting condom use in Africa "for selfish economic gain."

David Karanja, "Catholics Fighting AIDS,"
Catholic Insight, *March 2005.*

AIDS urges us to take a sharply negative view of the condom-distribution approach to the problem."

Even earlier, the bishops of the United States of America affirmed in their 1987 statement: "abstinence outside of marriage and fidelity within marriage as well as the avoidance of intravenous drug abuse are the only morally correct and medically sure ways to prevent the spread of AIDS."

I am quite concerned because people, especially the young, are misled when total protection is seemingly offered to them, while in fact there is no such total protection. Aware of the immensity of the pandemic, while at the same time maintaining the different but complementary levels of what is moral and what is merely hygienic, I wanted to speak out regarding the need not only to contain the continuous expansion of this pandemic, but also the need to prevent condom users from getting an infection that they previously thought was impossible to get.

Condoms Do Not Guarantee Protection from HIV

There are persons at risk of being contaminated, even though they think that their sexual relations, from the hygienic point of view, are totally safe. How many fall victim to this error? They would have taken a different attitude, at least to a certain extent, had they been given more valid and objective information. The reader is invited to reflect why, despite the invitation to promiscuity made by the "safe sex" campaign and the distribution of an enormous quantity of prophylactics where the pandemic is more widespread, the problem of infection has become even greater. . . .

Given that AIDS is a serious threat, any inadequate information based on false security offered by condoms used as prophylactics would be a grave irresponsibility. . . .

[A 2001 Workshop cosponsored by USAID, the FDA, the CDC, and the NIH focused] on the latex male condom for the prevention of HIV/AIDS and STDs during penile-vaginal intercourse. The Workshop Summary explains that available scientific evidence indicated that the condom reduces the risk of AIDS/HIV by 85%. There is then a 15% risk that remains.

The workshop also studied the transmission of other genital infections, and the usual conclusion is that studies demonstrated either *no or some protection* through condom use, or that there is *insufficient data to confirm* risk reduction. The diseases studied individually are the following: Gonorrhea, Chlamydial infection, Trichomoniasis, Genital Herpes, Chancroid, and Syphilis. The Human papillomavirus (HPV) is given some more attention, with the conclusion stating clearly that "[t]here was no evidence that condom use reduced the risk of HPV infection. . ." HPV is a very important STD associated with cervical cancer, which in the U.S. kills many more women than the HIV.

There is no such thing then as 100% protection from HIV/AIDS or other STD's through condom use. This data should not remain unnoticed, since many users, including youth, think that the condom provides total protection. . . .

Condom Use Increases the Risk of HIV/AIDS

That condoms do not provide total protection against the transmission of HIV and STD's is compounded by the fact the "safe sex" campaigns have led not to an increase in prudence, but to an increase in sexual promiscuity and condom use. In fact, there are studies showing that HIV/AIDS cases increase as the number of condoms distributed also increases. Human behavior is an important factor in the transmission of AIDS. Without adequate education aimed at abandoning certain risky sexual behavior in favor of well-balanced sexuality, as in pre-marital abstinence and marital fidelity, one risks perpetuating the pandemic's disastrous results. . . .

The Church does not propose the development of condoms with better quality that would assure 100% effectiveness against the transmission of HIV and STDs. What is being proposed is to live one's sexuality in a way that is consistent with one's human nature and the nature of the family. It has to be mentioned too that the WHO admits that abstinence and marital fidelity is a strategy *capable of completely eliminating* the risk of infection from HIV and other STDs; condoms, on the other hand, reduce the risk of infection.

Periodical Bibliography

The following articles have been selected to supplement the diverse views presented in this chapter.

Lawrence K. Altman   "AIDS Effort in Zambia Hailed as a Success," *New York Times*, August 14, 2006.

Natasha Bolognesi   "AIDS in Africa: A Question of Trust," *Nature*, October 12, 2006.

Erika Check   "AIDS Treatment: Staying the Course," *Nature*, August 10, 2006.

Bill Clinton   "The AIDS Crisis," *Vital Speeches of the Day*, November 2006.

Jon Cohen   "A Genetic Knack for Tackling HIV," *ScienceNOW Daily News*, July 19, 2007.

Geoffrey Cowley   "The Life of a Virus Hunter," *Newsweek*, May 15, 2006.

Geoffrey Cowley   "We Need to Change the Social Norms—Q&A: Why AIDS Is Still Spreading," *Newsweek*, August 17, 2006.

Richard Kim   "The People Versus AIDS," *Nation*, July 10, 2006.

Megan Lindow   "In Zambia, Treating the Symptom of Silence," *Chronicle of Higher Education*, September 1, 2006.

Roxanne Nelson   "AIDS Treatment Enters Its 25th Year," *Lancet Infectious Diseases*, August 2006.

Alexander Polier   "Safety in the Slums—A Play that Deals Frankly with AIDS Prevention and Treatment Is Changing Social Attitudes in Kenya," *Newsweek International*, April 9, 2007.

John Simons   "Crunch Time for an HIV Test," *Fortune*, May 29, 2006.

OPPOSING
VIEWPOINTS®
SERIES

CHAPTER 4

How Should AIDS Be Treated?

Chapter Preface

The Politics of Drug Trials

In order to develop effective AIDS treatments, medical research includes the process of conducting clinical drug trials, which are carefully controlled studies that enlist patients to take a new drug over time while being observed for results and possible side effects. Early in the AIDS epidemic, when death seemed imminent for anyone who was HIV-positive and patients had few options to combat the illness, many people with AIDS were eager to enroll in drug trials in order to access any treatment that might prolong their lives. The trend continues today, because drug trials give participants first access to new and better treatments. The meticulous and often slow process involved in getting Federal Drug Administration approval for new drugs has frustrated many people with AIDS. The tension created by the sense of urgency underlying AIDS research is aggravated by several controversies related to drug trials. Two of the most volatile issues include equal access to trials and the use of placebos in drug trials.

Some health care advocates take issue with the fact that the typical participant in any new drug trial is white and male. Women are often excluded from drug trials because women can become pregnant, and researchers do not want to be responsible for possible birth defects of an unborn child due to the untested drug. Poor people, as well, are often eliminated by drug researchers because they claim that dependence on public transportation and other public assistance makes economically challenged participants miss appointments more often than others. Whether by design or not, few people of color end up in drug trials unless a study specifically targets a racial or ethnic minority. Some attribute this to a lack of attention to diversity by researchers. Others point out that people of color are excluded because many studies are done in hospitals in white neighborhoods. Similarly, most drug trials are in large urban areas at hospitals affiliated with medical schools. This tends to discourage the participation of people who live in rural areas. The lack of equal access to drug trials leads some to conclude that drug trials limit the understanding of how drugs react in different types of bodies. Access also becomes extremely important when drug trials are a primary way to obtain treatment for an illness like AIDS.

In addition to equal access, the standard method of conducting drug trials by giving a control group a placebo (inactive substances against which test drugs are sometimes measured) has come under fire in clinical studies of AIDS. In order to have comparison data about a group of people who have not taken the drug under study, researchers typically give placebo doses to a portion of the participants in drug trials without revealing to the participants that they are not taking the drug under study. AIDS activists argue that it is unethical to use placebos in studies involving any group of seriously ill subjects. Medical researchers insist that placebo-controlled drug research is necessary to truly determine whether a drug is effective against AIDS. The debate has impeded AIDS research somewhat; researchers sometimes have found it difficult to fill studies that use placebos because many people with AIDS are willing to participate in drug trials only to try a new drug that may save their lives.

> "In plain English, AIDS drugs cause
> AIDS and death far more effectively
> than 'AIDS' itself."

AIDS Drug Treatments Are Deadly

Celia Farber

In the following viewpoint. Celia Farber charges that anti-AIDS drugs not only hit the wrong target—HIV, instead of the opportunistic diseases that make people sick—but are far more toxic than researchers and pharmaceutical companies are willing to admit, causing liver and kidney failure, heart attacks, and strokes. She concludes that HIV-antibody-positive people are better off avoiding anti-AIDS drug treatment. Celia Farber, a writer based in New York City, is the author of a collection of AIDS reporting, Serious Adverse Events.

As you read, consider the following questions:

1. According to AIDS doctor Roberto Giraldo, if HIV is not the true cause of AIDS, why do anti-HIV protease inhibitors have beneficial effects in AIDS patients?

2. What does the author describe as some of the potentially lethal effects of HAART therapy?

Celia Farber, "Drugs, Disease, Denial," *New York Press*, June 22, 2005. Reproduced by permission.

3. What death rates are actually being compared in misleading claims that today's drug regimens have dramatically reduced AIDS death rates, according to Farber?

The unified voice of the AIDS establishment has claimed thunderous victory for the post-1996 drug regimens that came to be known as "cocktails," which came into vogue about three years after death rates began declining, but nonetheless got full-trumpet credit for turning the tide.

Let me say, first, that I have been told and have reported and have imprinted upon my soul that for some people, at some stages of immune collapse, these drugs have helped, and maybe even prevented a slide into death. Roberto Giraldo, a doctor and expert in infectious and tropical diseases who crosses the world treating AIDS tells me this is probably due to their anti-oxidant, anti-viral and anti-microbial properties. He also tells me that in his experience, severe immune deficiency—which may be a more useful term than "AIDS"—occurs only where severe depletion of vital nutrients has occurred; reversing the illness starts with restoring those nutrients.

"Biochemically speaking, people who are malnourished, whether because they are poor, or because they are drug addicts, suffer from oxidization, and lack vitamins A, B, E, zinc and selenium. This is true of all AIDS patients I have ever seen," he said via telephone. "We cannot say that protease inhibitors are useless. In 1996 when they started to use protease inhibitors, there is no doubt that there was a change. Before 1996, all the people who used AZT, they were killed. There was no benefit there. Protease inhibitors—they are also very toxic—but they have benefits—they are antioxidants. No doubt they are poison and in the long run they kill the person, but you need proteases in the process of oxidation. Besides that, these drugs are also antibiotics." Giraldo believes that AIDS is a disease "of poverty," primarily, meaning [a disease] of extreme depletion of the cells, and that those who have been middle- or upper-class, who have gotten sick, [have] depleted their bodies through drug use and prolonged exposure to toxins. "HIV by itself causes nothing," he says. . . .

All Anti-HIV Drugs Are Potentially Lethal

Each of the 26 anti-HIV drugs currently on the market, combined in infinite combinations, or "cocktails," is, by admission of the manufacturers, potentially lethal. One of the unexpected effects of Protease Inhibitors, or so-called HAART therapy (Highly Active Antiretroviral Therapy), seen in recent years was a disruption of the body's fat-distribution mechanisms. This in turn (in addition to the fatty deposits on the upper neck and various parts of the body) has caused strokes and heart attacks in many patients, at the very moment when the drugs were theoretically "working," meaning so-called surrogate markers (cd4 cells and viral load) were going the right way. The other significant danger of HAART proved to be liver and kidney failure, which, according to a study done at the University of Colorado Health Sciences Center, "surpassed deaths due to advanced HIV," in 2002. In 2005 the *Wall Street Journal* reported that, according to a Danish study, AIDS drug cocktails "may double the risk of heart attacks." In 2004, the journal *AIDS* reported, with characteristic lack of alarm, "All 4 classes of antiretrovirals (ARVs) and all 19 FDA-approved ARVs have been directly or indirectly associated with life-threatening events and death." The paper was titled "Grade 4 Events Are as Important as AIDS Events in the Era of HAART," and "grade 4 events" referred to "serious or life-threatening events."

The conclusion: More than twice as many people (675) had a drug-related (grade 4) life-threatening event as an "AIDS event" (332). The most common causes of grade 4 events (drug toxicities) were "liver related." The greatest risk of death was not an AIDS "event" but a drug event—heart attacks ("cardiovascular events"). The authors wrote: "Our finding is that the rate of grade 4 events is greater than the rate of AIDS events, and that the risk of death associated with these grade 4 events was very high for many events. Thus *the incidence of AIDS fails to capture most of the morbidity experienced by patients with HIV infection [who are] prescribed HAART."* (Italics mine) In plain English, AIDS drugs cause AIDS and death far more effectively than "AIDS" itself.

HIV-Positive People Are Doing Well Without Drugs

Any triumph or victory claimed by the AIDS lobby for these drugs must be measured against a phenomenon they continue to deny exists, namely the untold number of people who are, to use their language, "living with HIV." This includes those invisible, uncounted, unloved people who are HIV-antibody positive, taking no drugs, not getting sick, not dying at a faster rate than HIV negatives. This begs the question of whether HIV causes AIDS. Currently, we have one camp—which I will call the "orthodoxy"—that argues that although current HIV drugs have frightful side effects and are difficult to take, they have nonetheless reversed a tide of death, which was seen throughout the 1980s and into the mid 1990s in people who were diagnosed with severe immune dysfunction. This camp, since it views AIDS as "HIV disease," meaning caused singularly by HIV, concentrates its efforts to "fight AIDS," on high-tech drugs that in various ways are meant to disable HIV in the blood. They are extremely mechanistic in their view of the human body and the immune system. It's all numbers. . . .

All people who question any facet of orthodox AIDS theory are "murderously irresponsible," and dripping with the psychic blood of millions. In this gladiatorial atmosphere, it is a wonder anybody speaks out at all. If only we could agree that most people are not, by nature, homicidal, and that dissenting views are productive to a search for truth, we might get somewhere. But I know, as surely as I know anything, that

The Controversy Over Nevirapine

A tragedy of global proportions is unfolding over a toxic anti-HIV drug given to hundreds of thousands of women and babies in the developing world in the belief that it can help prevent the spread of AIDS.

The drug, nevirapine, has become so central to AIDS agencies' efforts to support African and other developing nations that they are defending its use in dozens of poor countries, despite evidence that flaws in claims for its safety and effectiveness were covered up at the highest level by government scientists in the United States.

Nevirapine is acknowledged by Boehringer Ingelheim, its German manufacturer, to be capable of causing severe liver damage and life-threatening skin reactions soon after patients start taking regular doses. [In January 2005] a new warning about its dangers was issued by U.S. health officials. Deaths have been reported from several countries. . . .

Associated Press, the American news service, reported that top NIH [National Institutes of Health] officials, including [Anthony] Fauci, had been warned by an audit team that the study may have under-reported severe adverse events among the trial subjects, including at least 14 deaths. Researchers had also acknowledged that "thousands" of adverse events were not reported.

Neville Hodgkinson,
"Fresh Cause for Concern over the Side Effects of Nevirapine,"
Health Supreme, *January 30, 2005.*

my opponent in these pages will have characterized my position as "denialist." I am not denying anything. People have died of AIDS and the matter at hand is what they died from. A retroviral infection? A host of immuno-compromising factors? An absence of AIDS drugs—or indeed, the AIDS drugs themselves?

In 1984, when the US government announced at a press conference that one of its scientists—Robert Gallo—had found the "probable cause of AIDS," the official theory held that HIV caused AIDS by eating CD4 cells at a rapid clip. HIV was said to cause AIDS in a year or two, at best. Today, this theory has morphed into a range of possibilities; HIV causes AIDS in 10 to 15 years, in most people, but a small minority, so-called "long-term non-progressors," might be spared due to a genetic fluke.

Today's Drugs:
Deadly But Not as Bad as AZT

To my mind, if we are to stick to the orthodoxy's own measure, one cannot begin to speak of "saving" life until one has surpassed these ten or fifteen years. In the 1980s, AZT was claimed, with the same high dudgeon by the same orthodoxy, to "save" lives, yet few survived for more than a year on the earliest AZT regimens. The word "denial" comes to mind.

When people make dramatic claims for current drug regimens, the death rates they are actually comparing are not drugs vs. no drugs, but rather extremely toxic drugs of the early years compared to less toxic drugs of today. The earliest AIDS cases, marked by Kaposi's Sarcoma, were treated with chemotherapy (1981 to 1986) followed by AZT monotherapy in doses ranging from 1800 milligrams to 500 milligrams (1986 to 1989) followed by combinations of AZT, ddi, ddc and d4t (1989 to 1996) followed by protease inhibitors in various combinations, from 1996 to the present day. The one era I have no question resulted in deaths from the treatment itself, is the early AZT era, (circa 1986 to 1989) particularly when the common dosage was 1200 to 1800 milligrams. A German AIDS physician named Klaus Koehnlein told me in 2000, "We killed a whole generation of AIDS patients with AZT."

My friend Richard Berkowitz, author of *Stayin' Alive: The Invention of Safe Sex, A Personal History*, said: "Every friend I had that went on AZT in those early years is dead." He says that they lasted, on average, nine months on the drug. HIV positive since the early 1980s, Berkowitz credits his survival to two things: 1) having avoided AZT, and 2) safe sex.

What he means by "safe sex," a concept and term he himself developed and coined, together with the late activist Michael Callen, is far more complex than mere condom use. Drawing on the pioneering observations and warnings of Dr. Joseph Sonnabend, it involves an avoidance of many STDs and parasitic infections, coupled with a belief in life rather than a belief in the death sentence of HIV. Berkowitz has also mitigated my repudiation of cocktail therapy by stressing that a moderate regimen pulled him back from the brink of death.

> "AIDS denialists say that the risks of antiretrovirals outweigh their benefits. . . . Then why do people do better when they take more antiretrovirals?"

The Benefits of AIDS Drug Treatments Far Outweigh the Risks

Bob Funkhouser

In the following viewpoint, Bob Funkhouser cites numerous scientific studies that show highly active antiretroviral treatment (HAART) dramatically improves the health of people with HIV/AIDS and reduces prenatal HIV transmission. Funkhouser says AIDS-denialist critics of HAART cannot rationally answer two questions: If anti-AIDS drugs are more harmful than beneficial, why do AIDS patients improve when they take more antiretrovirals? And why do people who take antiretrovirals all the time do better than people who take them only occasionally? Bob Funkhouser is a technician in the theoretical division at Los Alamos National Laboratory in New Mexico. He is the cofounder of AIDSTruth.org, reflecting his primary interest in database-driven Web sites supporting HIV research.

Bob Funkhouser, "Benefits of Antiretrovirals Far Outweigh Their Risks," *aidstruth.org*, March, 2006. http://aidstruth.org. Reproduced by permission.

As you read, consider the following questions:

1. According to Funkhouser, in a survey of fifty-four anti-retroviral drug trials, how much was progression to AIDS or death reduced using a single drug, two drugs, and three drugs?

2. How do AIDS denialists distort the Concorde AZT trial results, according to the author? What were the actual results of Concorde?

3. What are the benefits of nevirapine, as cited by the author?

Numerous clinical trials as well as observational data (i.e. studies from clinical practice) have demonstrated beyond reasonable doubt that the benefits of antiretroviral treatment for people with HIV/AIDS far outweigh their risks. Antiretrovirals are an extremely well tested class of medicines. We present some of the evidence demonstrating that their benefits outweigh their risks here.

The current standard of care for people with HIV indicated for treatment, is a combination of three or more antiretroviral drugs taken everyday for life, known as Highly Active Antiretroviral Treatment (HAART). People with HIV generally do not need to begin antiretroviral treatment until their disease reaches an advanced stage. The World Health Organisation treatment guidelines for resource-limited settings explain when HAART should be commenced and what precise combination of antiretrovirals should be used. . . .

Antiretrovirals have also been shown to reduce the risk of women transmitting the virus to their infants. . . .

Clinical Trial Evidence

[A 2002] meta-analysis of 54 antiretroviral clinical trials has demonstrated that:

- Using one antiretroviral reduced progression to AIDS or death by 30% against placebo.

- Using two antiretrovirals reduced progression to AIDS or death by 40% against one antiretroviral.

- Using three antiretrovirals reduced progression to AIDS or death by 40% against two antiretrovirals.

AIDS denialists say that the risks of antiretrovirals outweigh their benefits. If this is the case, then why do people do better when they take more antiretrovirals? The denialists cannot rationally explain this.

[A 2006 NIH] randomised trial compared patients who took HAART continuously to patients who took structured treatment breaks. The rate of progression to AIDS or death in the continuous treatment arm was half the structured treatment break arm.

AIDS denialists say that the risks of antiretrovirals outweigh their benefits. If this is the case, then why do people who take antiretrovirals all the time do better than people who take them occasionally? The denialists cannot rationally explain this.

Evidence from Clinical Practice

Here are a small selection from the many studies from clinical practice that have shown HAART substantially reduces death and illness. Besides the studies shown here, HAART has been shown to reduce death and illness in Zambia, Hong Kong and Brazil.

One important study [published in 1998] demonstrated how effective HAART was in clinical practice. Quoting from the abstract:

Mortality among the patients declined from 29.4 per 100 person-years in 1995 to 8.8 per 100 person-years in the second quarter of 1997. There were reductions in mortality regardless of sex, race, age, and risk factors for transmission of HIV. The incidence of any of three major opportunistic infections (Pneumocystis carinii pneumonia, Mycobacterium avium complex disease, and cytomegalovirus retinitis) declined from 21.9 per 100 person-years in 1994 to 3.7 per 100 person-years by mid-1997. In a failure-rate model, increases in the intensity of antiretroviral therapy (classified as none, monotherapy, combination therapy without a protease inhibitor, and combination therapy with a protease inhibitor) were associated with stepwise reductions in morbidity and mortality. Combination antiretroviral therapy was associated with the most benefit. [our emphasis]

Using leading-edge statistical techniques, the author [of a 2005 study] calculated that the risk of progression to AIDS or death for patients on HAART in the Swiss Cohort was 14% of patients not on HAART. . . .

Concorde: A Trial Grossly Misrepresented by AIDS Denialists

AIDS denialists have claimed [in a 1994 study] that the Concorde trial supports the view that the risks of AZT outweigh its benefits. This is false.

Concorde was the biggest AZT monotherapy study over the longest period of time. But it showed unequivocally that AZT is not the cause of AIDS. Concorde only examined people with HIV WITHOUT symptoms of AIDS. It compared two strategies: Approximately half the trial participants took AZT immediately and the other half took placebo UNTIL they developed AIDS. Once patients progressed to AIDS, they were unblinded from the trial and given AZT. The participants taking AZT immediately had slower disease progression in the first year, but this dissipated with time resulting in no statistical difference in progression to AIDS. Since a large, approximately equal, number of participants in both arms progressed to AIDS, it clearly shows that AZT was no more harmful than placebo and therefore cannot be the cause of AIDS.

The denialists misrepresent the following about the Concorde trial: In a long-term follow up of the Concorde patients,

AIDS Drugs Have Saved 3 Million Years of Life in the United States

Per-person survival benefit, number of AIDS patients entering care, and era-specific and cumulative survival benefits

Year	Number of AIDS patients entering care	Percent surviving to next treatment era	Total survival benefit (Years)
1989–1992	158,370	33%	40,912
1993–1995	226,458	39%	460,465
1996–1997	72,716	86%	567,788
1998–1999	52,702	93%	582,359
2000–2002	71,946	91%	832,179
2003	24,780	—	330,189
Total			**2,813,892**

TAKEN FROM: R.P. Walensky et al., "The Survival Benefits of AIDS Treatment in the United States,"*Journal of Infectious Diseases,* June 1, 2006

those who deferred AZT treatment until they got AIDS were less likely (slightly, but statistically significantly) to die than those who took it immediately. But at this point the researchers were no longer comparing placebo against AZT.

As a scientist involved in the Concorde trial explained in an affidavit rebutting AIDS denialist Anthony Brink in a South African court case which Brink pulled out of, Concorde was not testing whether AZT was better than placebo; this was already known. It was only trying to determine whether AZT should be taken before one developed AIDS symptoms. It concluded that one should not.

If the patients in the placebo arm stayed on placebo and never took AZT when they got AIDS, then a comparison would have been possible (and we can conclude from the trials described above that such hypothetical patients would have done very badly). But this is not what happened: patients on placebo indeed started AZT treatment when they developed

AIDS because AZT had previously been shown unequivocally to be beneficial for people with AIDS.

Also, if the patients who took AZT immediately progressed to AIDS faster than the placebo group then one could conclude that AZT in patients without [HIV] symptoms is dangerous. But the study show the opposite result, albeit with reduced benefit over time.

We now know why taking AZT as a monotherapy before developing symptoms of AIDS was an unsuccessful strategy. Patients taking one antiretroviral develop a strain of HIV resistant to the virus in very short time (a few months on average). Consequently the drug stops destroying HIV and patients then experience the side-effects without the benefits. Then when they do eventually get AIDS, the drug no longer has a useful effect. With today's standard of triple-drug therapy, resistance takes, on average, a few years to develop, but resistance is probably not inevitable. When resistance happens, patients have to switch to a new antiretroviral regimen. The current medical consensus is that treatment should still be deferred until a CD4 count of between 200 and 350 or an AIDS-defining illness occurs.

It should also be noted that when AZT was originally prescribed as a monotherapy, it was prescribed in very high doses (1500mg per day). Nowadays it is prescribed in much lower doses (usually 500mg per day). . . .

Nevirapine

Clinical trials [demonstrated] the efficacy of nevirapine in reducing HIV viral load and increasing CD4 counts . . . , reducing mother-to-child transmission, . . . [and] [show that] "A single dose of nevirapine to the mother, with or without a dose of nevirapine to the infant, added to oral zidovudine prophylaxis starting at 28 weeks' gestation, is highly effective in reducing mother-to-child transmission of HIV."

> *"Between 10% and 30% of all new HIV infections . . . involve strains resistant to at least one anti-HIV drug."*

HIV Drug Resistance Is a Growing Concern

AIDSmeds.com

In the following viewpoint, the editors of AIDSmeds.com explain why even the most effective anti-AIDS drug treatments are increasingly compromised by HIV drug resistance. There is no way to prevent genetic mutations that occur during viral replication (which is very rapid in HIV) and produce new variants that partly or fully resist anti-AIDS drugs. AIDSmeds.com is an HIV/AIDS information and support Web site founded in 1999 by Peter Staley, a founding member of the AIDS activist group ACT-UP New York and a board member of the American Foundation for AIDS Research (AMFAR) from 1991 to 2004.

As you read, consider the following questions:

1. What two factors explain the high rate of mutations in HIV, as described by *AIDSmeds.com*?

2. According to the authors, how do three-drug regimens counter drug resistance?

AIDSmeds.com, "Understanding Drug Resistance," www.aidsmeds.com, May 5, 2006. Reproduced by permission.

3. How does drug treatment itself produce drug resistance, according to *AIDSmeds.com*?

HIV drug resistance means a reduction in the ability of a drug—or combination of drugs—to block HIV reproduction in the body.

Drug resistance occurs as a result of changes, or mutations, in HIV's genetic structure. HIV's genetic structure is in the form of RNA, a tight strand of proteins and enzymes needed by the virus to infect cells and produce new virus. Mutations are very common in HIV. HIV reproduces at an extremely rapid rate and does not contain the proteins needed to correct the mistakes it makes during copying.

Two of the most important HIV enzymes are reverse transcriptase and protease. Nucleoside analogues—also called Nucleoside Reverse Transcriptase Inhibitors (NRTIs)—and Non-Nucleoside Reverse Transcriptase Inhibitors (NNRTIs) target the reverse transcriptase enzyme. Protease Inhibitors (PIs) target the protease enzyme.

Another important protein is gp41, which is found out on the outer coat—the envelope—of HIV. This protein is the target of Fuzeon® (enfuvirtide; T-20), an anti-HIV drug that was approved in 2003. Fuzeon prevents HIV from binding to healthy T-cells in the body, which prevents these T-cells from becoming infected with the virus.

In order for these anti-HIV drugs to be effective, they must first attach themselves to the necessary enzyme. Certain mutations can prevent a drug from binding with the enzyme and, as a result, make the drug less effective against the virus.

HIV drug-resistance mutations can occur both before and during anti-HIV drug therapy. . . .

Resistance by Natural Selection

Soon after HIV enters the body, the virus begins reproducing at a rapid rate (approximately 10 billion new viruses are produced every day). In the process, HIV produces both perfect copies of itself (wild-type virus) and copies containing errors (mutated virus). In other words, the body doesn't carry just one type of virus, but actually carries a large population of mixed viruses called quasi-species.

When HIV reproduces, it wants to be wild-type virus. This is the most natural and powerful form of the virus and, as a result, reproduces the best. Before anti-HIV therapy is started, wild-type virus is the most abundant in the body and dominates all other quasi-species.

When HIV makes mistakes during copying, mutated viruses—called variants—are produced. Some variants are too weak to survive and/or cannot reproduce. Other variants are strong enough to reproduce but are still not able to compete with the more fit wild-type virus. In turn, their numbers are less than wild-type virus in the body.

Some variants have mutations (sometimes called polymorphisms) that allow the virus to partly, or even fully, resist an anti-HIV drug. This is why HIV-positive people should never take just one anti-HIV drug (monotherapy). For example, HIV only requires one mutation in the reverse transcriptase enzyme—called "M184V"—to become completely resistant to Epivir® (3TC) and Emtriva® (emtricitabine). The same problem holds for the non-nucleoside reverse transcriptase inhibitors Viramune® (nevirapine), Rescriptor® (delavirdine), and Sustiva® (efavirenz). The "K103N" mutation can cause the virus to become highly resistant to these drugs. . . .

These HIV mutations occur randomly and there is no proven way to prevent them from occurring. Variants containing these mutations usually don't go on to develop additional mutations; doing so compromises their ability to stay alive in the body. Thus, while these variants may be completely resistant to one anti-HIV drug, they are almost always sensitive to other drugs used in a regimen. This is why three-drug regi-

Better New Drugs, Less New Resistance

As the inevitable consequence of the incomplete suppression of HIV-1 replication by antiretroviral drugs, resistance is a permanent threat for patients who are undergoing antiretroviral treatment, and transmission of resistant viruses is becoming an important concern. Prevention of resistance is a priority that requires unrelenting patient education regarding the risks of resistance and the use of improved drug regimens that ensure optimal tolerance, adherence, and potency. Once established, resistance evolves, diversifies, and may become irreversible. Nonetheless, new drugs are becoming, available that appear to retain substantial antiviral activity against HIV-1 strains that are resistant to multiple drugs. These are either drugs from existing classes that have increased potency and improved pharmacokinetic properties or drugs from new classes that are not susceptible to cross-resistance. Although preliminary data indicate that viral resistance to these new drugs can also develop, the lessons learned about the development of viral resistance to the currently available antiretroviral drugs may prove helpful in devising treatment strategies with optimized antiviral potency that can minimize the development of resistance to these new agents.

François Clavel and Allan J. Hance, "HIV Drug Resistance,"
New England Journal of Medicine, *March 4, 2004, pp. 1023–35.*

mens work better: a variant may be resistant to one of the drugs but doesn't stand much of a chance when facing two other drugs that bind to different parts of the same enzyme or different parts of the virus.

Transmission of Drug-Resistant Virus

Many HIV-positive people now take anti-HIV drugs. If someone has developed resistance to one or more of these anti-

HIV drugs and has unprotected sex or shares needles with someone who is not infected with the virus, it is possible that they can infect their partner with a drug-resistant variant—a strain of HIV containing mutations that cause resistance to one or more anti-HIV drugs. . . .

According to some studies, between 10% and 30% of all new HIV infections—defined as people infected with HIV over the past two years—involve strains resistant to at least one anti-HIV drug. To make matters worse, many researchers expect that this percentage will increase in the years to come, and that many more people will become infected with strains of HIV resistant to multiple drugs.

It might also be possible for someone who is already infected with HIV to be infected, again, with a drug-resistant strain of HIV. This is sometimes referred to as "reinfection" or "superinfection."

Resistance Acquired During Treatment

Soon after anti-HIV drug treatment is started, the amount of virus in the body is reduced dramatically. Unfortunately, no anti-HIV drug—or combination of drugs—is able to completely stop HIV from reproducing. In other words, there is always a small population of virus in the body that continues reproducing, despite the presence of anti-HIV drugs. . . .

Anti-HIV drug therapy reduces the amount of all HIV quasi-species in the body. The amount of wild-type virus is dramatically reduced and the number of variants is also decreased.

Even though wild-type virus is the most natural and powerful form of HIV, it is the most sensitive to anti-HIV drugs. Because of this, HIV variants in the body have a survival advantage over that of wild-type virus. In the presence of anti-HIV drug therapy, variants can become the dominant strain of HIV, even though there is a much smaller amount of HIV in the body.

Over time, variants accumulate additional mutations. Some of these mutations will harm the virus while others will further limit a drug's ability to stop it from reproducing. Once the virus has accumulated enough mutations, the anti-HIV drugs lose their ability to bind to it and prevent it from reproducing. As the drugs become weaker, the amount of drug-resistant virus in the body increases, causing an undetectable viral load to become detectable again and increase over time. Should the drug-resistant virus continue to reproduce, it can acquire even more mutations to resist the anti-HIV drugs completely.

Mutations that emerge during therapy can be divided into two groups: primary mutations and secondary mutations. Each anti-HIV drug is associated with at least one primary mutation. This mutation is of greatest concern, as they are the ones that cause the greatest amount of drug resistance. Secondary mutations do not cause drug resistance unless a primary mutation is present. If both primary and secondary mutations are present, drug resistance can become more complicated.

While primary and secondary mutations can cause the virus to become resistant to anti-HIV drugs, they usually have a negative effect on the power of the virus. This is why some people who are experiencing an increase in their viral load might not see a decrease in their T-cell counts, at least not initially. In other words, the virus loses its ability to cause damage to the immune system if it contains drug-resistance mutations. However, some studies have shown that certain primary and secondary mutations can cause the virus to regain its power and, quite possibly, become even more powerful than wild-type virus. In turn, most experts recommend switching therapies before the virus accumulates any additional mutations.

Cross-resistance can also occur during therapy. When HIV becomes resistant to one drug, it can automatically become resistant to other drugs in the same class. For example, the primary and secondary HIV mutations that occur in someone who is taking the NNRTI Sustiva are the same mutations that cause resistance to the NNRTI Viramune. Even though the person hasn't yet taken Viramune, he or she will likely be cross-resistant to the drug and will not likely benefit from it.

"Nutritional and natural health approaches—not toxic ARV drugs—are the answer to the AIDS epidemic."

Alternative Nutritional AIDS Treatments Are Safe and Effective

Matthias Rath and Aleksandra Niedzwiecki

German physician Matthias Rath and his Polish biochemist colleague Aleksandra Niedzwiecki argue in the following viewpoint that AIDS is caused by malnutrition, not HIV; that the pharmaceutical industry conspires to disseminate toxic AIDS drugs to vulnerable populations out of greed; and that the true cure for AIDS-related illness is vitamin therapy and other nutritional supplements. Rath and Niedzwiecki are codirectors of the Rath Health Foundation, dedicated to opposition to established medical and scientific views of HIV as the cause of AIDS.

As you read, consider the following questions:

1. Why is the pharmaceutical industry pushing AZT and other anti-AIDS drugs on African AIDS victims, according to the authors?

Matthias Rath and Aleksandra Niedzwiecki, "The Natural Control of AIDS," Dr. Rath Health Foundation, December 2005. Copyright © by Dr. Rath Health Foundation. Reproduced by permission.

2. Why do the authors applaud South Africa's leadership in the fight against HIV/AIDS?

3. How do vitamins and other micronutrients overcome AIDS, in Rath and Niedzwiecki's opinion?

The pharmaceutical industry is not a 'health industry' but an 'investment industry' that makes money not from the prevention of diseases—but from their expansion. In recent years, scandal after scandal around the drug industry revealed its true nature to everyone as reckless profiteers at the expense of the health and lives of millions of people. The pharmaceutical industry within our society behaves like a cancer in our body: it grows at the expense of the body and eventually kills it. . . .

Africa Has Become the Dumping Ground for Toxic AIDS Drugs

Realizing that they are about to lose their multibillion-dollar investments in cancer and heart disease drugs the pharmaceutical 'business with disease' has turned its attention to the AIDS market and the developing world.

The drug manufacturers and their agents have banked on South Africa and the rest of the continent being largely ignorant about the fraudulent nature of the pharmaceutical business. Over the past decades the pharmaceutical multinationals—the drug cartel—has turned South Africa and the entire African continent into a dumping ground for their toxic ARV [anti-retroviral] drugs. AZT and other ARV drugs are 'chemo' drugs that are being used on AIDS victims because the 'chemo' market with cancer is about to collapse globally.

Some of these ARVs, like Boehringer's Viramune (nevirapine) have proven to be so toxic that they harm and kill people and are not allowed to be given to mothers and their babies in other countries—not even in Boehringer's home country Germany. The people of Africa truly have been abused by the drug multinationals as experimental 'guinea pigs'. But this time is over now!

'AIDS Inc.' and Its Disastrous Impact on South African Society

In order to promote their unscrupulous 'business with disease' inside South Africa, the drug multinationals have strategically undermined and infiltrated all sectors of society. The management of socially responsible organizations has naively invested their funds into the pharmaceutical drug business and become financially dependent on this 'business with disease'. For example, 'leaders' of the Congress of South African Trade Unions (COSATU) have invested tens of millions of rands from the pension funds of millions of COSATU members in pharmaceutical multinationals and drug companies via its investment arm. Did these COSATU 'leaders' duly inform their members about the fraudulent nature of the pharmaceutical 'business with disease'? Many COSATU members are AIDS victims themselves—did they give their approval to take their money for helping to spread ineffective and toxic drugs? This information answers the question for millions of COSATU members, why some individuals in the present COSATU leadership consistently attack their own government on its steadfast position to provide effective and safe solutions to the AIDS epidemic. But not only is COSATU compromised by the interests of the drug cartel. Members of other community organizations in South Africa must also ask themselves: Whom do our leaders serve by protecting the pharmaceutical 'business with AIDS' and by attacking our own government for trying to save lives?

Courageous Stand of the South African Government

The South African government is a global leader in the fight against the HIV/AIDS epidemic and in its resistance to pharmaceutical interests pushing ARV drugs. The harder our government is being attacked by the mass media under pressure from the multibillion-dollar drug business, the more the people need to support our government.

Alternative AIDS Treatments

Dietary supplements are commonly used in an effort to boost the immune system. Foods or substances derived from foods (garlic, Chinese bitter melon, and turmeric) are used, as well as nonfood dietary supplements such as shark cartilage or blue-green algae (spirulina). Vitamins, minerals, and amino acids are also used in an attempt to boost the immune system.

"Dietary Management of AIDS-HIV,"
Life Positive, *2006.*

Our Minister of Health, Dr. Tshabalala-Msimang, has every reason for her public warnings in connection with ARV drugs. The side effects of these toxic drugs have become the leading cause of death among AIDS patients taking ARV drugs! According to the statistics of the National Department of Health in the Western Cape Province, 5 out of every 100 patients treated with ARVs are dead within 3 months, rising to 8 out of every hundred after 6 months. After 1 year on these drugs, 13 out of every hundred are dead. These facts once and for all destroy the fairy-tale of the drug business and their stakeholders in the mass media that ARVs are the answer to the AIDS epidemic.

Clearly the time has arrived for natural, effective, safe and affordable alternatives to the fraudulent investment business with ineffective and toxic ARV drugs.

Since the Dr. Rath Health Foundation started its work in South Africa, it has been focusing on exposing the unscrupulous pharmaceutical 'business with disease'—[a business that is conducted] at the expense of the health and lives of millions of AIDS patients. It was this exposure of the genocidal proportions of the pharmaceutical 'business with disease' that put the pharmaceutical cartel and its stakeholders in South

Africa in a state of sheer panic. The mass media have been running amok against the Foundation for one reason only—because it exposed the genocide by the drug companies.

The pharmaceutical stakeholders in South Africa are panicking about the billions in financial losses and the possible meltdown of their entire industry. And they have every reason to be afraid: pharmaceutical executives, as well as their stakeholders in pharmaceutical medicine, the media and other sectors will be held accountable by the law.

Soon millions of people in South Africa will have recognized the genocidal dimension of this pharmaceutical fraud business, that they have been robbed of their health and their money and that they were forced to sacrifice their husbands, wives, children to these business interests. Once that happens, the people will make sure that those responsible will be held accountable for their crimes in the courts of law. And that day is not far off!

But this exposure is only part of the work of the Dr. Rath Health Foundation. Being the world leader in the field of natural cancer research, the Foundation decided to support the South African government in winning the fight against AIDS with effective and safe natural means. It is a well known fact that vitamins and other micronutrients boost the immune system and help fight immune deficiencies, including AIDS. This knowledge has been suppressed and even fought by the pharmaceutical stakeholders for decades, because vitamins are not patentable and—unlike ARVs—do not yield huge profits.

Community Vitamin Programmes
Document the End of the AIDS Epidemic

Towards this end, the Dr. Rath Health Foundation has been donating vitamin programmes to community organizations for nutritional support of people living with AIDS. Already the results of the first 18 participants were so dramatic that the Foundation published them on May 6, 2005, in the world's most influential newspaper, the *New York Times*, under the sobering title "Stop the AIDS-Genocide by the Drug Cartel!" New York is the seat of the United Nations and from there the news reached the four corners of the world.

After these encouraging results, SANCO extended the vitamin community programme to hundreds of people with even more encouraging results. In December 2005, the time had come to summarize the health benefits of these initial community health programmes from the townships of Cape Town and bring them to the attention of community organizations nationwide.

Vitamins Can Reverse AIDS

Vitamins can reverse even severe symptoms of AIDS, and increase quality of life and life expectancy. In the absence of a cure for HIV/AIDS, nutritional and natural health approaches—not toxic ARV drugs—are the answer to the AIDS epidemic, [and] everyone [should] understand why the pharmaceutical industry and their stakeholders in medicine, the media and the street peddlers of the drug cartel—like the TAC—are panicking. All of them now know that no longer will profits counted in billions of rands continue to fill the chests of the drug companies at home and abroad.

The scientific facts ... fully confirm the position of the South African government in its stand on natural health approaches in the fight against AIDS. The representatives of SANCO, NAPWA, THO and the Dr. Rath Foundation unanimously called on the South African government to intensify its worldwide leadership in the implementation of natural and traditional medicine into the national health care system. All speakers applauded the courageous stance of the Minister of Health, Dr. Tshabalala-Msimang and assured her of their future support. Based on the facts documented here, it is time for the people of South Africa to come out in strong support for their government and its natural approach to health. Now it is time to educate as many people as possible on the new possibilities to fight AIDS and other diseases and maintain health naturally. Each one must teach one!

> "*People with AIDS whose improving
> condition had been attributed . . . to
> nutritional supplements had been on
> [antiretroviral drugs] all along.*"

Alternative Nutritional AIDS Treatments Are Deadly Quackery

Ian Hodgson

In Africa, where the World Health Organization (WHO) initiative to provide 3 million people with antiretroviral HIV/AIDS drugs (ARVs) fell short by 1.8 million, and where there is a strong tradition of folk medicine, skepticism takes a backseat when someone promises a miracle cure for AIDS, says Ian Hodgson in the following viewpoint. Hodgson argues that the best-known proponent of the so-called natural approach, Matthias Rath, is unethically promoting his vitamin supplements without evidence that they work, unethically conducting treatment trials in Cape Town, South Africa, and unscrupulously recruiting treatment recipients. Worst of all, Hodgson contends, Rath is urging sick people to reject ARVs, whose effectiveness is beyond question. Ian Hodgson, a lecturer at the University of Bradford in West Yorkshire, England, researches and writes about cultural perceptions of HIV and international AIDS policy.

As you read, consider the following questions:

1. According to Hodgson, what is the difference between the demand for ARVs in South Africa and the supply of ARVs there?
2. What two charges of Rath's, though exaggerated, have a "kernel of truth," according to the author?
3. How does the Treatment Action Campaign, cited by Hodgson, characterize Rath and his nutritional supplement theory?

HIV has always been more than simply a virus: wherever it strikes there is controversy, panic, and confusion. In 2005, heated debate around aid allocation policy, and the morality of certain HIV prevention strategies were prominent in the discourse. As always, access to AIDS treatments was also high on many agendas, not least because December 2005 marked the end of the World Health Organisation's "3x5" initiative: a two-year campaign to provide 3 million people globally with antiretroviral medication (ARVs).

The campaign fell short of its target by about 1.8 million, and this deficit highlights another major controversy that continues to blight AIDS care provision and treatment in South Africa. The country with the most people infected with HIV is paradoxically also the place where there seems to be most controversy. In 2000, President Thabo Mbeki publicly questioned links between HIV and AIDS, aligning himself with a small group or largely United States-based AIDS denialists. Now, Dr Matthias Rath, perhaps the most controversial nutrition-specialist since Robert Atkins, seems to have the ear of South Africa's health minister, Mantombazana Tshabalala-Msimang.

Matthias Rath's Dangerous Alternative

Matthias Rath is a German-born medical researcher who over the years has gained increasing prominence as one of a growing number of scientists who challenge orthodox views of the HIV epidemic and the treatment of affected people. According to Rath, antiretroviral medications (ARVs) for AIDS are harmful and essentially ineffective; their endless promotion by drug companies and international agencies is simply a product of economics and corporate greed.

Instead, he promotes a nutritional alternative through which, the Rath Foundation website claims, "millions of lives can be saved now—naturally." This "natural" approach is a cocktail of vitamin supplements, amino acids, minerals and trace elements that the Rath Foundation claims are able to reverse the symptoms of AIDS Rath cites empirical evidence supporting his view of ARVs and of the benefits of a nutritional approach. Through 2005 he has been putting on show people with AIDS who have apparently eschewed ARVs in favour of the Rath approach, with dramatic results. In a country where the demand for ARVs outstrips supply by a factor of four, news of an alternative is for some miraculous.

A Firestorm of Criticism

Rath has attracted a firestorm of criticism from scientists, activists, and academic institutions whose work he claims justifies his theories. The Harvard School of Public Health for example, famously distanced itself from Rath in May 2005, after he cited findings from a study in Tanzania published by the school as confirming his views. Harvard, in a press statement, said: "We condemn these irresponsible and misleading statements as in our view they deliberately misinterpret findings from our studies to advocate against the scale-up of antiretroviral therapy."

On various fronts, Rath has been accused of opportunism, hypocrisy, of being a charlatan, and trading on AIDS misery.

The Treatment Action Campaign (TAC), a highly vocal and influential NGO [nongovernmental organization] in South Africa, which for years has advocated that the 600,000 or so affected people still without medication gain more access to ARVs, accuses Rath of promoting pseudo-science.

At the end of November 2005, in an action supported by the South African Medical Association, TAC sued the government for not taking a more robust stance against Rath's activities in the country and demanded a report from the health minister, Mantombazana Tshabalala-Msimang. This action is a clear indication of increasing concern not just over the theories promoted by the Rath Foundation, but also over allegedly unethical trials in Cape Town's townships, and unscrupulous recruitment of treatment recipients. This accusation was given some credibility recently when, according to one news report in October 2005, two people with AIDS whose improving condition had been attributed by the Rath Foundation to nutritional supplements, had been on ARVs all along.

Science, Relativism, and South Africa

The refusal of the South African government to condemn Rath outright has caused widespread consternation: indeed, the health minister has appeared with Rath, and seems to go out of her way to promote the benefits of nutrition—food "just like our grandmothers used to make"—to maintain the health of people living with HIV/AIDS.

Why has this situation come to such a point? Two considerations are important in understanding and learning from this debacle: the possibility that the issues at stake may simply be a matter of perspective (that, in other words, Rath could have a point), and that the controversy could be the product of political and economic expediency.

Questioning Treatments
Is Not in Itself Wrong

The first consideration may on the surface have some merit. Science and the community have never been easy bedfellows.

Desperate People Latch On to Quack Cures

At the only hospital in the capital of this tiny West African nation [of Gambia], a 3-year-old AIDS patient named Suleiman receives his daily dose of medication—a murky brown concoction of seven herbs and spices served out of a bottle that once contained pancake syrup.

The boy is told a spoonful a day will make him better. His mother, Fatuma, takes the same concoction, as do several dozen other AIDS and HIV patients here. Adults take two spoonfuls.

"It's amazing," Fatuma says. "Two weeks ago, I was very ill, weak and couldn't eat without vomiting."

This has become the treatment for HIV/AIDS patients here since early January, when Gambian President Yahya Jammeh announced he had discovered a cure for the disease that has wreaked havoc across Africa. He made that announcement in front of a group of foreign diplomats, telling them the treatment was revealed to him by his ancestors in a dream. . . .

Health officials worldwide remain doubtful of these claims. Experts also say it's in places like Gambia that the poor and desperate will latch onto anything resembling hope.

"For a country's leader to come up with such an outlandish conclusion is not only irresponsible, but also very dangerous, and he should be reprimanded and stopped from proclaiming such nonsense," said Professor Jerry Coovadia of the University of Kwa Zulu Natal in South Africa.

Jeff Koinange, "In Gambia, AIDS Cure or False Hope?"
CNN.com, March 17, 2007.

The "transitional truth" of science—an assumption that today's theories may be discounted tomorrow, and that "truth" is generally in a state of flux—never rests easy with a public who desire certainty, especially in a context so sensitive and charged as HIV/AIDS.

The nutrition versus ARV debate could be an example of the usual rough and tumble of the adversarial world of scientific discourse, taking place in the public domain instead of behind the closed door of a laboratory. Overt criticism of Rath—beyond the context of scientific debate—could therefore be premature. . . .

Rath's accusation of the predatory behaviour of the drug companies that manufacture ARVs also has a kernel of truth. Drug companies *are* often responsible for maintaining high prices, and holding onto drugs patents for as long as possible: Brazil's government went head-to-head with the pharmaceutical company Abbott in July 2005 in a bid to wrestle the patent of ARV Kaletra from the company, in order to provide a cheaper generic alternative.

The year 2005 also saw vigorous spats at the World Trade Organisation and G8 over proposed (though not as yet fully realised) flexibilities on trade-related intellectual property rights (Trips) in relation to ARVs, confirming that rules of trade are not readily eschewed for public-health imperatives

But the Effectiveness of ARVs Is Beyond Question

However, the credibility of the notion that Rath is simply a victim of an inflexible and over-bearing scientific community breaks down over his foundation's recommendation that people with AIDS use nutritional support in *place* of ARVs, rather than the more orthodox view that the two can be part of a holistic package of care. The sheer number of studies— from a range of sources—that demonstrate the benefit of ARVs, suggest that any position that does not include these must be challenged; and by the criteria of the "transitional truth" notion, Rath has produced no substantial data yet to justify outright rejection of ARVs. Rath therefore cannot and should not make the claims he does.

The second consideration in this drama, that the sluggishness of the South African government in condemning Rath may have ulterior political and economic motives, also has evidence to draw on. A policy that implicitly supports a nutritional alternative to ARVs could distract attention from the appalling lack of progress in access to AIDS medications. The roll-out of ARVs in South Africa is painfully slow: this is the wealthiest and one of the most stable nations on the continent, yet of the 840,000 people who require ARVs, estimates for the end of 2005 suggest that only around 200,000 (up from 104,000 in September 2004) will have access.

The "dash" for ARVs that started in the 1990s has created immense problems for South Africa economically. But it has also become a matter of national pride: why *should* developed countries dictate to South Africa about how it should tackle HIV? The health minister, speaking of "3X5" in June 2005, stated that "nobody had asked South Africa" what they thought of the proposal; instead it was imposed from Geneva. Seeking an African solution to an African problem has for South Africa been implicit in a number of policy developments: and the emphasis on nutrition could be one example.

| "Tuberculosis—an airborne disease—is the leading cause of death among people who are HIV-positive."

Treating Tuberculosis Is Critical in AIDS Interventions

Office of the U.S. Global AIDS Coordinator

In the following viewpoint, the federal Office of the U.S. Global AIDS Coordinator outlines the alarming incidence of tuberculosis (TB) in people infected with HIV—one-third of the 40 million people who are living with HIV/AIDS. The AIDS coordinator advocates routine screening for TB, cross-screening for HIV at TB clinics, and expanded access to adequate treatment for both TB and HIV. The Office of the U.S. Global AIDS Coordinator is the office of the Department of State charged with implementing the President's Emergency Plan for AIDS Relief (PEPFAR), a five-year, $15-billion program established in 2004 to combat AIDS around the world.

As you read, consider the following questions:

1. According to the Office of the U.S. AIDS Coordinator, what percent of AIDS-related deaths are caused by TB in sub-Saharan Africa, where the AIDS epidemic is concentrated?

Office of the U.S. Global AIDS Coordinator, "Critical Interventions: Tuberculosis and HIV/AIDS," U.S. Department of State, July 2006.

2. How is the Fenote Tesfa Project in Ethiopia designed to improve TB surveillance and treatment, according to the AIDS coordinator?

3. How has PEPFAR successfully improved TB treatment rates in Kenya, according to the author?

Tuberculosis (TB)—an airborne disease—is the leading cause of death among people who are HIV-positive. Approximately one-third of the nearly 40 million people living with HIV/AIDs are also infected with TB. In areas such as sub-Saharan Africa, up to half of AIDS-related deaths are caused by TB. Of those people living with HIV/AIDS with latent TB infection, approximately 10 percent per year develop active TB. It is vital to treat people with TB to prevent illness and death, as well as to prevent the spread of TB to others.

The U.S. President's Emergency Plan for AIDS Relief (Emergency Plan/PEPFAR) supports national TB and HIV/AIDS programs that integrate HIV prevention, treatment, and care activities into TB services, including support for TB care and treatment.

The priorities for HIV/TB interventions are:

• Routine screening for TB disease;

• HIV counseling and testing for clients at TB facilities;

• Diagnosis and treatment of people living with HIV/AIDS with active TB using DOTS [Directly Observed Treatment]; and

• Ensuring that cross-referrals are made for TB patients to adequate care and treatment for HIV/AIDS, including antiretroviral treatment and cotrimoxazole.

The Emergency Plan also supports the development of laboratory infrastructure for the diagnosis of opportunistic infections, including TB. Support for diagnostic laboratories is focused on a public health approach that includes the development of tiered laboratory networks linked through an external quality assurance system.

Because of the high rate of co-morbidity between TB and HIV/AIDS, the U.S. Government urges counseling and testing facilities to screen for signs of TB, and offer HIV counseling, testing and referral for TB diagnosis and treatment. Diagnostic HIV testing and counseling of TB patients allows those who test HIV-positive to be referred for HIV/AIDS treatment and other services. PEPFAR supports development of a comprehensive curriculum and training materials to improve TB/HIV surveillance in TB clinics. The U.S. Government has developed two "basic preventive care packages," including one for adults and one for children aged 0–14 born to HIV-infected mothers. These packages support national HIV/AIDS strategies and are for use by U.S. Government in-country staff and implementing partners. They outline interventions, including TB screening and TB treatment therapies, [that] target the primary causes of HIV-related illness and death.

International Interventions

The following are a few examples of how the Emergency Plan is working under national strategies and in partnership with host nations to support TB services for people living with HIV/AIDS:

In Ethiopia, Fenote Tesfa Project, a private sector program, provides employees with access to TB care and treatment at their company's clinic. Prior to the Fenote Tesfa Project, few Ethiopian parastatal clinics provided TB treatment. In October 2004, the Fenote Tesfa Project initiated a workplace HIV/TB program. Healthcare professionals now receive training on TB and HIV management in collaboration with the Ethiopian Ministry of Heatth. One beneficiary of the program explained: "When I was told that my problem is TB, I was thinking about the referrals and the expenses I may have to incur to go daily to a health center to get treatment. But [my

Outbreaks of Extensively Drug-Resistant Tuberculosis

At the beginning of 2005, extensively drug resistant tuberculosis (XDR-TB) was detected in KwaZulu-Natal and has highlighted the lethal combination of HIV and TB in South Africa, where an estimated 60% of TB patients overall are also HIV-infected.

Of the 53 persons initially diagnosed with XDR-TB at a district hospital in the KwaZulu-Natal province, from January 2005 to March 2006, 44 tested for HIV and each of them was found to be HIV-positive. Mortality was very high: 52 of the patients died within, on average, a month of initial sputum collection. By early October 2006, XDR-TB had been identified at 33 health-care facilities across KwaZulu-Natal.

TB drug resistance arises mainly because of inadequate TB control, poor patient or clinician adherence to standard TB treatment regimens, poor quality drugs or inadequate drug supplies. People living with HIV are particularly vulnerable to developing drug-resistant TB because of their increased susceptibility to infection and progression to active TB.

This outbreak underscores the need to rapidly ensure prompt TB diagnosis and effective TB treatment for persons living with HIV in order to prevent drug resistance from developing and spreading. Access to TB culture and drug sensitivity testing must be improved, and effective infection control practices must be introduced in HIV care clinics to prevent the spread of TB.

UNAIDS and WHO, "AIDS Epidemic Update:
Special Report on HIV/AIDS," December 2006, p. 12.

doctor] told me that the service is available onsite at the clinic, and thanks to the [Fenote Tesfa] Project, I have already started taking my drug on the day I was diagnosed. I am following my course here at the workplace receiving counseling by my own company medical doctor."

In Vietnam, the U.S. Government supports efforts to establish HIV diagnostic counseling and testing in TB clinics and improve screening of TB and referral to TB services among HIV-positive persons. The U.S. Government developed protocols for TB/HIV, which were approved by the Ministry of Health of Vietnam, along with a program needs assessment completed by the Vietnam National TB Program. Training materials on HIV diagnostic counseling and testing in TB programs were developed and have been translated, reviewed and approved by the Vietnam National TB Program.

In Uganda, The AIDS Support Organization (TASO) is providing comprehensive, holistic care using a clinic- and home-based model of service delivery. To meet the care needs of isolated communities, TASO has integrated prevention, care and treatment services. TASO's efforts are providing outlying populations with comprehensive clinical care. TASO's integrated care package includes screening for active TB and treatment for TB/HIV co-infection. By providing treatment for HIV-positive patients with TB disease and with latent TB infection, TASO has helped improve overall health among program beneficiaries and reduce mortality rates.

In Guyana, the U.S. Government and an Emergency Plan partner have been actively engaged in a Guyanese Ministry of Health initiative to improve TB and TB/HIV care. The PEPFAR partner organization's activities have focused on improvement in TB laboratory capacity, diagnosis, and clinical care. In addition, they are assisting the Ministry of Health with the revision of their five-year strategic plan for TB.

In Kenya, the Eastern Deanery of the Nairobi Catholic Diocese has provided health care through seven clinics in the eastern slums of Nairobi since the early 1990s. In 2001, integrated HIV and TB services were established in these clinics. Initially, TB patients were referred to freestanding counseling and testing centers; however, only one-in-eight patients referred for counseling and testing actually sought testing. With Emergency Plan support, the program began in 2004 to routinely offer on-site HIV counseling and testing to all outpatients believed to have TB. Nurses now conduct testing, using simple HIV rapid tests done in the patient's presence. Of the 1,917 patients offered HIV counseling and testing over 19 months, 85 percent accepted treatment during their initial clinic visit—and nearly all of those who came for a follow-up due to active TB eventually accepted testing.

Periodical Bibliography

The following articles have been selected to supplement the diverse views presented in this chapter.

Karla Adam	"An Old Foe Gains Strength—New Fears of Killer TB" *Newsweek*, September 13, 2006.
Asia Pacific Biotech News	"Thailand's HIV/AIDS Treatment Could Serve as a Model for Other Countries," August 30, 2006.
Hayden Bosworth	"The Importance of Spirituality/Religion and Health-Related Quality of Life Among Individuals with HIV/AIDS," *Journal of General Internal Medicine*, December 2006.
Holly Burkhalter	"The Politics of AIDS," *Foreign Affairs*, February 2004.
Daniel Engber	"Three Pills? I Only Want One!" *Slate*, July 13, 2006.
Jim Frederick	"Asia's Quest for an AIDS Vaccine," *Time International*, September 30, 2002.
Kenslea Ged and Lori Yeghiayan	"AIDS Treatment Goes Global," *USA Today Magazine*, March 2006.
Peter Hawthorne	"Dying to Get AIDS Drugs to All," *Time International*, April 28, 2003.
Roger Thurow	"In Kenya, AIDS Therapy Includes Fresh Vegetables," *Wall Street Journal*, March 28, 2007.
Tiffany C. Veinot, et al.,	"Supposed to Make You Better but It Doesn't Really: HIV Positive Youths' Perceptions of HIV Treatment," *Journal of Adolescent Health*, March 2006.
Diane Weathers	"A Battle Worth Fighting," *Essence*, December 2004.
Kathryn Williams	"AIDS Official: 'We've Made Progress,'" *Newsweek*, February 24, 2005.

For Further Discussion

Chapter 1

1. In this chapter, what kind of evidence is used to support arguments that AIDS is a serious and growing threat to humankind? On the other hand, what kind of evidence is used to ground the arguments that claim the threat of AIDS is exaggerated? Do certain kinds of evidence convince you more than others?

2. After reading the viewpoints in Chapter 1, consider which countries and which populations are hardest hit by the AIDS epidemic. Why do you think some communities experience more devastation from AIDS than others?

Chapter 2

1. Before reading the selections in Chapter 2, what preconceptions did you have about the causes of AIDS? What viewpoint(s) most challenged your assumptions? Why?

2. Rob Noble argues that the standard scientific method is the most reliable way to determine the cause of AIDS. Christine Maggiore argues that science isn't always failsafe. Which argument is strongest? Support your answer using examples from the viewpoints.

Chapter 3

1. The debate over safer-sex education vs. abstinence-based prevention programs is contentious in America today. What values do abstinence programs aim to promote? Do you share those values? If not, what values are more important to you?

2. The Community HIV/AIDS Mobilization Project argues that HIV testing infringes on individual civil rights. Do

you agree? How can testing programs be designed to protect the privacy of those who seek to be tested for HIV? Is it more important to learn who is HIV-positive through testing, or to preserve each individual's civil rights?

Chapter 4

1. In this chapter, viewpoints by Farber, AIDSmeds.com, and Rath and Niedzwiecki present evidence that drug treatments for AIDS have serious drawbacks. List the various disadvantages involved in drug therapy. Compare your list to the drug-related benefits cited in the viewpoints by Funkhouser and Hodgson. Do you think drug therapy is the best way to treat AIDS? Why or why not?

2. Traditional medicine is sometimes at odds with alternative medicine in recommending treatment for AIDS. What alternative medical treatments do Farber and Rath and Niedzwiecki propose? What evidence do they use to support the use of these alternative treatments? What role do you think alternative treatments should play in treatment programs for people with AIDS?

Organizations to Contact

The editors have compiled the following list of organizations concerned with the issues debated in this book. The descriptions are derived from materials provided by the organizations. All have publications or information available for interested readers. The list was compiled on the date of publication of the present volume; names, addresses, phone and fax numbers, and e-mail and Internet addresses may change. Be aware that many organizations take several weeks or longer to respond to inquiries, so allow as much time as possible.

AIDS Vaccine Advocacy Coalition (AVAC)
101 W. Twenty-third St., #2227, New York, NY   10011
(212) 367-1084
e-mail: avac@avac.org
Web site: www.avac.org

AVAC is a community- and consumer-based organization founded in 1995 to accelerate the ethical development and global delivery of vaccines for HIV/AIDS. The organization provides independent analysis, policy advocacy, public education, and mobilization to enhance AIDS research. It also provides the AVAC Update Newsbook, "Community Perspective in Research, Advocacy, and Progress."

Alive & Well AIDS Alternatives
11684 Ventura Blvd., #338, Studio City, CA   91604
(877) 411-AIDS • fax: (818) 780-7039
e-mail: info@aliveandwell.org
Web site: www.aliveandwell.org

Alive and Well AIDS Alternatives challenges popular beliefs and theories about HIV and AIDS. It sponsors clinical studies and scientific research in an attempt to verify the central tenets about the disease, its cause, and its treatments. The organization also publishes the book *What If Everything You Thought You Knew About AIDS Was Wrong?*

238

American Foundation for AIDS Research (AmFAR)

733 Third Ave., 12th Floor, New York, NY   10097
(212) 682-7440 • fax: (212) 682-9812
Web site: www.amfar.org

The American Foundation for AIDS Research supports SIDS prevention and research and advocates AIDS-related public policy. It publishes several monographs, compendiums, journals, and periodic publications, including the *AIDS/HIV Treatment Directory*, published twice a year, the newsletter *HIV/ AIDS Educator and Reporter*, published three times a year, and the quarterly *AmFAR Newsletter*.

American Red Cross AIDS Education Office

1709 New York Ave. NW, Suite 208, Washington, DC   20006
(202) 434-4074
e-mail: info@usa.redcross.org
Web site: www.redcross.org

Established in 1881, the American Red Cross is one of America's oldest public health organizations. Its AIDS Education Office publishes pamphlets, brochures, and posters containing facts about AIDS. These materials are available at local Red Cross chapters. In addition, many chapters offer informational videotapes, conduct presentations, and operate speakers bureaus.

Center for Women Policy Studies (CWPS)

1221 Connecticut Ave. NW, Suite 312
Washington, DC   20038
(202) 872-1770 • fax: (202) 296-8962
e-mail: cwps@centerwomenpolicy.org
Web site: www.centerwomenpolicy.org

The CWPS was the first national policy institute to focus specifically on issues affecting the social, legal, and economic status of women. It believes that the government and the medical community have neglected the effect of AIDS on women and that more action should be taken to help women who have AIDS. The center publishes the book *The Guide to Resources on Women and AIDS* and produces the video *Fighting for Our Lives: Women Confronting AIDS.*

Centers for Disease Control and Prevention (CDC)
National AIDS Clearinghouse, PO Box 6303
Rockville, MD   20849-6303
(800) 448-0440 • fax: (301) 519-6616
e-mail: ContactUs@aidsinfo.nih.gov
Web site: http://aidsinfo.nih.gov

The CDC is the government agency charged with protecting the public health by preventing and controlling diseases and by responding to public health emergencies. The CDC National AIDS Clearinghouse is a reference, referral, and distribution service for HIV/AIDS-related information. All of the clearinghouse's services are designed to facilitate the sharing of information and resources among people working in HIV/AIDS prevention, treatment, and support services. The CDC publishes information about the disease in the *HIV/AIDS Prevention Newsletter* and the *Morbidity and Mortality Weekly Report.*

Family Research Council
700 Thirteenth St. NW, Suite 500, Washington, DC   20005
(202) 393-2100 • fax: (202) 393-2134
e-mail: corrdept@frc.org
Web site: www.frc.org

The Family Research Council promotes the traditional family unit and the Judeo-Christian value system. The council opposes the public education system's tolerance of homosexuality and condom distribution programs, which its members believe encourage sexual promiscuity and lead to the spread of AIDS. It publishes numerous reports from a conservative perspective, including the monthly newsletter *Washington Watch* and bimonthly journal *Family Policy.*

Global AIDS Interfaith Alliance (GAIA)
The Presidio of San Francisco
San Francisco, CA   94129-0110
(415) 461-7196 • fax: (415) 41-9681
e-mail: info@thegaia.org
Web site: www.thegaia.org

GAIA is a nonprofit organization composed of top AIDS researchers and doctors, religious leaders, and African medical officials, most of whom are associated with religiously based clinics and hospitals. The organization is concerned with infrastructure development and the training of prevention educators and personnel to conduct HIV testing and counseling. It also emphasizes the modification of values, structures, and practices that predispose women and girls to higher HIV infection rates than men, that stigmatize ill persons, and that contribute to public denial. GAIA's Web site offers news and updates about AIDS.

Health, Education, AIDS Liaison (HEAL)
(416) 406-HEAL
e-mail: inquiries@healtoronto.com
Web site: www.healtoronto.com

HEAL is a network of international chapters that challenges the validity of the traditional HIV/AIDS hypothesis and the efficacy of HIV drug treatments. HEAL believes that debate and open inquiry are fundamental parts of the scientific process and should not be abandoned to accommodate the theory of HIV. Its Web site provides articles that question the link between HIV and AIDS and offers information about HIV tests, AIDS in Africa, and drug treatments.

**Joint United Nations Programme
on HIV/AIDS (UNAIDS)**
20 Ave. Appia, Geneva 27   CH-1211
   Switzerland
(4122) 791-3666 • fax: (4122) 791-4187
e-mail: unaids@unaids.org

Web site: www.unaids.org

UNAIDS is a joint United Nations program on HIV/AIDS created by the combination of six organizations. It is a leading advocate for worldwide action against HIV/AIDS, and its global mission is to lead, strengthen, and support an expanded response to the AIDS epidemic that will prevent the spread of HIV, provide care and support for those infected and affected by HIV/AIDS, and alleviate the socioeconomic impact of the epidemic. UNAIDS produces many publications, including *HIV/AIDS Human Resources and Sustainable Development,* and *Young People and HIV/AIDS: Opportunity in Crisis.*

National AIDS Fund
1030 Fifteenth St. NW, Suite 860, Washington, DC   20005
(202) 408-4848 • fax: (202) 408-1818
e-mail: info@aidsfund.org
Web site: www.aidsfund.org

The National AIDS Fund seeks to eliminate HIV as a major health and social problem. Its members work in partnership with the public and private sectors to provide care and to prevent new infections in communities and in the workplace by means of advocacy, grants, research, and education. The fund publishes the monthly newsletter, *News from the National AIDS Fund,* which is also available through its Web site.

National Association of People with AIDS (NAPWA)
1413 K St. NW, Washington, DC   2005-3442
(202) 898-0414 • fax: (202) 898-0435
e-mail: napwa@thecure.org
Web site: www.napwa.org

NAPWA is an organization that represents people with HIV. Its members believe that it is the inalienable right of every person with HIV to have health care, to be free from discrimination, to have the right to a dignified death, to be adequately housed, to be protected from violence, and to travel and immigrate regardless of country of origin or HIV status. The association publishes several informational materials such as an annual strategic agenda and the annual *Community Report.*

Rockford Institute
934 N. Main St., Rockford, IL 61103
(815) 964-5053
e-mail: rkfdinst@bossnt.com
Web site: www.rockfordinstitute.org

The Rockford Institute seeks to rebuild moral values and recover the traditional American family. It believes that AIDS is a symptom of the decline of the traditional family, and it insists that only by supporting traditional families and moral behavior will America rid itself of the disease. The institute publishes the periodicals *Family in America* and the *Religion & Society Report* as well as various syndicated newspaper articles that occasionally deal with the topic of AIDS.

Bibliography of Books

Books

Gregory F. Barz   *Singing for Life: HIV/AIDS and Music in Uganda.* New York: Routledge, 2006.

Arthur M. Fournier   *The Zombie Curse: A Physician's 25-Year Journey into the Heart of the AIDS Epidemic in Haiti.* Washington DC: Joseph Henry, 2006.

John G. Bartlett   *A Pocket Guide to Adult HIV/AIDS Treatment.* Rockville, MD: Department of Health and Human Services, 2005.

Robert E. Beckley and Jerome R. Koch   *The Continuing Challenge of AIDS: Clergy Responses to Patients Friends, and Families.* Westport, CT: Auburn House, 2002.

Greg Behrman   *The Invisible People: How the U.S. Has Slept Through the Global AIDS Pandemic, the Greatest Humanitarian Catastrophe of Our Time.* New York: Free Press, 2004.

Hanson Bourke   *The Skeptic's Guide to the Global AIDS Crisis.* Colorado Springs, CO: Authentic, 2006.

Rhidian Brook — *More Than Eyes Can See: A Nine Month Journey Through the AIDS Pandemic*. London: Marion Boyars Publishers, 2007.

Michel Cochran — *When AIDS Began: San Francisco and the Making of an Epidemic*. New York: Routledge, 2003.

Rebecca Culshaw — *Science Sold Out: Does HIV Really Cause AIDS?* Berkeley, CA: North Atlantic Books, 2007.

Harold D. Foster — *What Really Causes AIDS?* Victoria, B.C., Canada: Trafford Publishing, 2006.

Brett Grodeck and Daniel S. Berger — *The First Year: HIV: An Essential Guide for the Newly Diagnosed*. New York: Marlowe, 2007.

Emma Guest — *Children of AIDS: Africa's Orphan Crisis*. London: Pluto Press, 2003.

Anne C. Conroy, ed. — *Poverty, AIDS, and Hunger: Breaking the Poverty Trap in Malawi*. New York: Palgrave Macmillan, 2006.

Susan S. Hunter — *AIDS in Asia: A Continent in Peril*. New York: Palgrave Macmillan, 2005.

John Iliffe — *The African AIDS Epidemic: A History*. Athens, OH: Ohio University Press, 2006.

Alexander C. Irwin, Joyce Millen, and Dorothy Fallows — *Global AIDS: Myths and Facts, Tools for Fighting the AIDS Pandemic*. Cambridge, MA: South End Press, 2003.

Robert Klitzman and Ronald Bayer	*Mortal Secrets: Truth and Lies in the Age of AIDS*. Baltimore, MD: Johns Hopkins University Press, 2005.
Stephen Lewis	*Race Against Time: Searching for Hope in AIDS-Ravaged Africa*. Berkeley, CA: Publishers Group West, 2006.
Maureen E. Lyon and Lawrence J. D'Angelo	*Teenagers, HIV, and AIDS: Insights from Youths Living with the Virus*. Westport, CT: Praeger Publishers, 2006.
Alexander Rodlach	*Witches, Westerners, and HIV: AIDS and Cultures of Blame in Africa*. Walnut Creek, CA: Left Coast Press, 2006.
David A. Ross	*Preventing HIV/AIDS in Young People*. Geneva, Switzerland: World Health Organization, 2006.
Eileen Stillwaggon	*AIDS and the Ecology of Poverty*. New York: Oxford University Press, 2006.

Index

A

Abstinence and Behavior Change for Youth program (USAID), 167–168

Abstinence programs, 136

  are effective in stemming spread of AIDS, 166–173

  fail to halt global HIV epidemic, 174–180

ACT UP (AIDS Coalition to Unleash Power), 15–17

Activism, AIDS, 14–15

  outreach to black communities and, 65–66

Adolescents, HIV screening for, 157–158

Adventist Development and Relief Agency (ADRA), 167–168

Africa. *See* Sub-Saharan Africa; *specific countries*

African Americans

  AIDS is a crisis among, 59–67

  as target of HIV-mediated genocide, 121–122

  women, AIDS infection among, 20

AIDS (acquired immune deficiency syndrome)

  case rate in U.S., by race/ethnicity, 63

  first report of, 13

  HIV virus is cause of, 86–94

  HIV virus is not cause of, 95–101

  indicator diseases for, 33

  is a crisis in black America, 59–67

  per-person survival benefits from treatment, by era, 260

  perception as male disease, 19

AIDS epidemic

  abstinence programs have failed to halt, 174–180

  Catholic Church must oppose use of condoms to halt, 186–190

  Catholic Church should endorse use of condoms to halt, 181–185

  high-risk groups for, 25–26

  high-risk regions for, 23–25

  is exaggerated, 32–41

  possibility of, in China, 68–73

American Red Cross (ARC), 168

Antiretroviral drugs/therapy

  benefits outweigh risks, 202–208

  effectiveness is beyond question, 227–228

  potential dangers of, 197–198

  production of, in China, 81

  South African opposition to, 217–219

  in sub-Saharan Africa, 47

  years of life saved by, 206t

Asia, HIV epidemic trends in, 27–28

Atkins, Harold, 63–64

Avoiding Risk, Affirming Life project (Catholic Relief Services), 168

AZT, 16

  benefits outweigh risks, 205–207

  as dangerous drug, 200–201

recommended HIV screening for pregnant, 157

Women in the New Millennium (Moletsane and DeLancey), 20

World Relief, 172–173

Y

Youth and Children with Health Options Involving Community Engagement Strategies (Y-CHOICES) program (Pact), 170

Z

Zhiyong Fu, 77